In Louisiana it is not uncommon to see Protestant Christians in their churches on Sunday morning and, come nightfall, to find them in the Spiritist churches getting help for their problems.

— Reverend Ray T. Malbrough

An Insider's Guide to This Magico-Religious System

Throughout the ancient world, people presented offerings to the deities along with petitions and prayers. Most often they were supplicated with a bonfire or flame from an oil lamp.

In time, Christianity pushed the ancestral deities into the background. Within the religious systems of Santeria, Condomble, and Voudun, people began to worship their gods under the guise of Christian saints. The saints took on characteristics of the pagan deities. Special days of the week were assigned to them, along with a candle of a particular color, and rulership over certain problems and occupations. This belief in the saint's ability to intercede on the petitioner's behalf continues to this day, in a magico-religious system that the Christian church refers to as "popular religiosity."

In this book, you will find a guide to seventy-four saints and their attributes. Learn how to evoke the saints for practical help in your life through prayer, candle burning, and divination.

D0897519

ABOUT THE AUTHOR

Reverend Ray T. Malbrough's first book, *Charms, Spells & Formulas,* has been a perennial favorite with readers. At the time he wrote it, he had only a tenth-grade education. Eleven years after leaving school, Ray enrolled in a nursing school and worked in that profession for three years to gain the medical knowledge he uses in his counseling. Since then he has worked continuously as a spiritual reader, helping people solve their problems. He studied comparative religion as well as Wicca, spiritualism, shamanism, voodoo, and Santeria, and became an ordained minister. In 1993 he founded All Saints Chapel of Faith Church in Baton Rouge, Louisiana. As holder of the church seal, he is the only minister who can ordain new ministers as diviner priests or priestesses. He has initiated and trained two Wiccan covens, and is one of only a few Wiccan high priests who can legally marry couples in the state of Louisiana. He also assists other religious groups such as Voodoo and Wiccans in gaining state recognition as legal religions.

TO WRITE TO THE AUTHOR

If you wish to contact the author or would like more information about this book, please write to the author in care of Llewellyn Worldwide, and we will forward your request. Both the author and publisher appreciate hearing from you and learning of your enjoyment of this book and how it has helped you. Llewellyn Worldwide cannot guarantee that every letter written to the author can be answered, but all will be forwarded. Please write to:

Reverend Ray T. Malbrough
Llewellyn Worldwide Ltd.
P.O. Box 64383, Dept. K456–1, St. Paul, MN 55164-0383, U.S.A.

Please enclose a self-addressed, stamped envelope for reply, or $1.00 to cover costs. If outside U.S.A., enclose international postal reply coupon.

THE
MAGICAL POWER
OF THE
SAINTS

EVOCATIONS & CANDLE RITUALS

REVEREND RAY T. MALBROUGH

1998
Llewellyn Publications
St. Paul, Minnesota, 55164-0383, U.S.A.

FIRST EDITION
Second Printing, 1998

Cover Design by Lisa Novak
Cover Photo: Leo Tushaus
Editing and Interior Design by Connie Hill
Permission granted by Roman, Inc. for use of images of Our Lady of Grace, St. Francis of Assisi, St. Therese of Lisieux, and the Infant of Prague © 1989 Roman, Inc. Permission granted by Northwind Picture Archives for use of images of Our Lady of Lourdes, St. Cecelia, St. Bartholomew, St. Benedict, St. Ignatius Loyola, St. Paul, and St. Michael. Permission granted by Mary Evans Picture Library for use of images of Our Lady of Mercy and St. Expedite.

Library of Congress Cataloging-in-Publication Data
Malbrough, Ray T., 1952–
        The magical power of the saints : evocations & candle rituals / Ray T. Malbrough. — 1st ed.
        p.   cm.
    Includes bibliographical references and index.
    ISBN 1–56718–456–1 (trade paper)
    1. Christian patron saints—Miscellanea.   2. Magic   3. Blessing and cursing.   4. Divination.   5. Candles and lights.   6. Holy oils. I. Title.
BF1623.C47M35   1998
133.4'4—dc20   98-19622
                                                                  CIP

Llewellyn Publications
A Division of Llewellyn Worldwide, Ltd.
St. Paul, Minnesota 55164-0383, U.S.A.

Printed in the U.S.A.

DEDICATION

In memory of my father, Lawney Mark Malbrough Sr., whose spirit is giving help and inspiration to the children he deserted as infants in real life. Now he is free to work out his karmic debt from the spirit world, through his guidance.

In memory of Scott D. Cunningham: may his spirit have refreshment, light, and peace until the time of his reincarnation.

ACKNOWLEDGMENTS

Special thanks to Raymond Buckland, whose teaching of witchcraft has immensely added to the church's study of comparative religion. His inspiration helped me form my church, the First Church of Celtic and Saxon Wicca.

In grateful thanks to Carl and Sandra Weschcke, and the staff at Llewellyn, for their patience with me.

And also thanks to the other Llewellyn authors whose books are providing a wider field of study for potential ministers of our church: Ted Andrews, Timothy Roderick, D. J. Conway, Kenneth Johnson, D. Jason Cooper, Diane Stein, Douglas Monroe, Amber Wolfe, Raven Grimassi, Silver Raven-Wolf, Edain McCoy, Donald Tyson, Edred Thorsson, Cyndi Dale, Dr. Jonn Mumford, Tony van Renterghem, Patricia Telesco, Konstantinos, Donald Michael Kraig, Pauline and Dan Campanelli, Ed Fitch, Kveldulf Gundarsson, Richard Webster, Kisma K. Stepanich, and Gwydion O'Hara for his stories on mythology.

CONTENTS

Chapter 10

Chapter 11

INTRODUCTION

T he contents of this book will be controversial to some, a welcome and blessing to others, and condemned as heresy by some religious leaders. The practices described here are a spiritual form that has developed outside of conventional religion. These teachings embrace a spiritual culture and beliefs forming a tradition from several different sources merged into one. Here is a rich spirituality, very much alive, that is a blend of religion and folk magick. It illustrates many elements of ancient beliefs still practiced to this day, practices that conventional religion has in vain tried to blot out. When conventional religion fails the people, they will seek out alternative ways to solve their problems.

All the folk spells in this book are traditional. Now, folk spells can be a bit tricky—what works for one person may not work for another. In this case, divination is used to see what will work. The proper role of divination is explained in full, as it has always been used by leaders within the magico-religious culture. True divination is not done to entertain or to satisfy curiosity—it is not a parlor game. The proper function of divination is to gain divine knowledge that will guide the practitioner in solving the difficulties encountered in daily living. Its proper function is to warn people of mistakes they may be making that could worsen the conditions they find themselves in. Divination will guide an individual to the right path leading to the fulfillment of their destiny in this life, for a diviner priest or priestess must be honest and tell the person if their desire is not what is best for them. A true diviner will not tell the person what they want to hear, just to keep them coming back with their money, as many so-called psychic readers will do.

Also within these pages, methods of exploitation will be exposed, such as the practice of charging exorbitant prices for services rendered by diviners. The belief that paying a high price for something means you are getting the best is based on a lie. Anyone who shops the department stores should know that many stores will sell the same brand of items. For example, one store may have the brand and model of refrigerator you are looking for selling for $800, and another will have the same brand on sale for $675. You will undoubtedly buy from the store you trust, one that is not taking advantage of you with an inflated price. You want to have the same relationship with a diviner—to know you can put your faith in their integrity.

Chapter 1

Deities and Saints

hroughout the ancient world, offerings were presented to the deities, along with supplications and prayers. Most often the deities were supplicated with fire—be it a bonfire or the flame from an oil lamp—while prayers were offered. Supplicating the saints for help is a carryover from the practice of honoring the heroes of myth in ancient cultures as well as remembering the dead.

Ancient religions were predominantly magico-religious in structure. Their priesthood was expected to have a knowledge of magical practice and of the myths on which their faith in a God or Goddess was based. Within the myths, the ancient deities became anthropomorphized, having rulership over certain areas of life and nature.

Early Christian priests and clergy were stiff competitors of an already established religion. Unable to eradicate all elements of the indigenous religions, Christians canonized some deities as saints. Saint Ann corresponds with Dana/Danu/Ana/Anu, and Saint Brigit of Kildare with the Goddess Brighid. Saint Tathan/Tatheus and Saint Hubert are the Christian version of Cernunnos, whose emblem was the stag. The laity saw similarities between the stories of the lives of the saints and the symbols or attributes of ancient deities.

As ancient deities were pushed further into the background, the number of Christian saints increased, beginning with the martyrs. Many miracles and miraculous cures from disease occurred after believers invoked help from a deceased martyr, or merely came in contact with the body or clothing of a martyr. This strengthened the continued practice of ancestor worship and cults of the dead. The belief that these people who had died had gone to heaven, dwelling with God and at the same time having supernatural powers, began to slowly replace belief in the ancient deities.

Equating an ancient deity with a Catholic saint also became a common practice among African descendants in the New World. Within the Afro-magico-religious systems of Santeria, Condomble, and Voudun, people continued to worship their ancestral deities under a new guise.

In time devotions to the saints began to take on many similarities to the worship of pagan deities. Special days of the week were assigned to them, as well as a certain colored candle, and rulership over specific areas of life's problems. The saints became patrons of various occupations and trades.

Popular religiosity had transformed the Christian saints into figures with the same status as the ancient deities. Belief continues to this day in the saints' ability to intercede on behalf of those who invoke their aid.

The Catholic Church has always taught that the saints are our friends in heaven. Vatican Council II addressed this in the document, Constitution on the Church, No. 50: "It is supremely fitting, therefore, that we love those friends and coheirs of Jesus Christ, who are also our brothers and extraordinary benefactors, that we render due thanks to God for them and suppliantly invoke them and have recourse to their prayers, their power and help in obtaining benefits from God through His Son, Jesus Christ."

The prayers of worshippers are often directed to a saint or deity, and, as a member of the religion, petitioners' desires are often obtained. When the prayers accompany an offering to the saint or deity, the action becomes religious magic, very similar to the magico-religious practices throughout the pre-Christian world. This religious magic, which the Roman Catholic Church calls "popular religiosity," is very similar to the magico-religious practices of many so-called primitive cultures in the world today.

In the magico-religions, the practice of giving an offering to a saint or deity is considered payment for services rendered. An offering is required for every request made. You are giving first in order to receive in return. Part of the thinking that develops within a magico-religious practice is that only a thief would expect to get something for nothing.

In families and cultures that practice regular devotion to the saints, children are given the names of particular saints in the hope that the saint will watch over and protect the child. This is similar to magico-religious thinking where a child is born under the rulership of a particular deity in the culture's pantheon. These deities are considered the spiritual parents of the child and they will assist him or her in the affairs of their life. The saint or deity, in effect, becomes a spiritual ally for the person.

The fact that magico-religious practices are successful is what makes them a threat, especially to Protestant Christianity. In Louisiana it is not uncommon to see many Protestant Christians in their churches on Sunday morning—but come nightfall, they will be seen in the Spiritist Churches getting help for their problems.

There is a firm belief in the magico-religious culture that a deity, saint, or spirit will directly intervene and give aid with one's problems. The pagan deities and spirits are actually anthropomorphized astral forces of the universe, emanating from the Creator God, and corresponding to the material and emotional temperament of the culture. The saints, on the other hand, belong to the realm of the "Mighty Dead," dwelling with deity in the upper world. So we see that a saint is not the same as an ancient deity or spirit.

The Catholic Church teaches that a place called purgatory exists, where the souls of the just who died with the stains of sin are cleansed by expiation before they are admitted to heaven. The Church defines purgatory as the state or condition under which the faithful departed undergo purification.

Honoring and remembering your ancestors is another aspect of magico-religious practices. Christians have no difficulty petitioning the help of the saints, who were once flesh and blood as we are, but died hundreds of years ago. The Church has always maintained that you should pray for deceased family members. The Church teaches: "Although the souls in purgatory cannot merit, they are able to pray and obtain the fruit of prayer. The power of their prayers depends on their sanctity. It is certain that they can pray and obtain blessings for those living on earth. They are united with the pilgrim Church in the Communion of Saints."

Much has been written in the past illustrating the assimilation of African deities with Catholic Saints, but we will not explore this here. The following section describes the saints and the attributes that have become associated with them in popular religiosity.

THE DIVINE CHILD

THE INFANT JESUS ➤
OF PRAGUE

Feast day: December 25
Day of the week: Monday
Color of candle: Orange
    or red

Petition in matters of health,
surgeries, special requests,
guidance and wisdom.

THE INFANT JESUS
OF ATOCHA

Feast day: December 25
Day of the week: Monday
Color of candle: Gold or
    yellow

Petition for help in any
situation, strength in sickness,
to keep lawsuits away, to
delay a lawsuit in the courts.

VISIONS OF THE BLESSED MOTHER

OUR LADY OF FATIMA ➢

Feast Day: May 13
Day of the week: Tuesday
Color of candle: White

Petition for protection from evil, the wrath of adversaries, freedom from binding situations, against the harm of evil spirits.

⪡ OUR LADY OF GRACE

Feast day: January 21
Day of the week: Friday
Color of candle: Blue

Petition concerning special requests, calming anger in another, fidelity in marriage, finding love.

OUR LADY OF GUADELUPE ➤

Feast day: December 12
Day of the week: First day of
    each month
Color of candle: Pink, white,
    or three colors: green,
    white, and red.

Petition for matters concerning peace, sickness, help in any situation, luck for the month.

Patroness of Mexico and the Americas.

OUR LADY OF CHARITY

Feast day: September 8
Day of the week: Saturday
Color of candle: Yellow

Petition for protection of home and family, return of love, to bring a new lover, money and prosperity.

OUR LADY HELP OF CHRISTIANS

Feast day: August 1
Day of the week: Monday
Color of candle: Blue

Petition for special requests, in times of sickness, to surmount difficulties, during times of war.

OUR LADY OF THE ➤ IMMACULATE CONCEPTION

Feast day: December 8
Day of the week: Monday
Color of candle: White

Petition for assistance in sickness, health, for fertility.

Patroness of the United States and Brazil.

➤ OUR LADY OF LORETTO

Feast day: December 10
Day of the week: Saturday
Color of candle: White

Petition for help when looking for a place to live such as an apartment or home, for protection when traveling by air, for peace in the home.

Patroness of home builders and aviators.

OUR LADY OF LOURDES ➤

Feast day: February 11
Day of the week: Wednesday
Color of candle: White

Petition in times of sickness, to regain health, for special favors.

➤ OUR LADY OF MERCY

Feast day: Sept. 24
Day of the week: Sunday
Color of candle: White

Petition for peace, health, needed justice, release from jail.

Our Lady of the Miraculous Medal ➤

Feast day: Nov. 27
Day of the week: Wednesday
Color of candle: Blue and
    white

Petition her aid in restoring health, for bad habits broken, special favors, to avert danger, protection of motorcyclists, blessings bestowed.

Our Lady of Hope

Feast day: August 1
Day of the week: Thursday
Color of candle: Blue

Petition for peace, to stop harassment from enemies, protection in times of war.

Our Lady of Perpetual Help

Feast day: March 7
Day of the week: Sunday
Color of candle: White or blue

Petition for protection of children, special requests.

◄ OUR LADY OF REGLA

Feast day: September 7
Day of the week: Friday
Color of candle: Blue

Petition for protection of young children, health, money problems, fertility.

OUR LADY OF MOUNT CARMEL (DEL CARMEN)

Feast day: July 16
Day of the week: Saturday
Color of candle: White or
    brown

Invoke for protection from accidents or sudden death, special requests.

Patroness of Chile.

OUR LADY OF PROMPT SUCCOR

Feast day: August 1
Day of the week: Saturday
Color of candle: Gold

Petition in epidemics, sickness, for special requests, to bring about quick change, help for the poor and needy.

Patroness of the State of Louisiana.

THE FEMALE SAINTS

SAINT AGNES ➤

Feast day: January 21
Day of the week: Friday
Emblem: A lamb
Color of candle: White or
   blue

Invoke her for problems
concerning fidelity in marriage, to find a suitable mate,
sincerity in relationships.

◄ SAINT ANN/ANNE/ANA

Feast day: July 26
Day of the week: Monday
Color of candle: White

Petition for special requests,
help for the deaf and blind.

Patroness of cabinet makers,
Canada, grandmothers,
housekeepers, housewives,
mothers, women in labor.

SAINT BARBARA ➤

Feast day: December 4
Day of the week: Saturday
Emblem: A twer
Color of candle: Red

Petition her to drive away evil, as a protector of women, for love problems, when in-laws are trying to break up a marriage, gambling luck, to clear your path of obstacles, help to release someone in prison, protection during storms.

Patroness of ammunition workers, architects, artillery, brass workers, builders, fireworks, fortifications, gunners, impenitence, lightning, minors, prisoners, stone masons, storms, warehouses.

SAINT MARIA GORETTI

Feast day: July 6
Day of the week: Friday
Color of candle: Pink

Petition her concerning fidelity in marriage, help in abusive relationship, pardon from the death penalty.

SAINT BRIGID (BRIDE) OF KILDARE ➤

Feast Day: February 1
Day of the week: Sunday
Emblem: A cow
Color of candle: Yellow

Petition for childbirth, protection from fires, fertility, the hearth, healing, physicians, agriculture, animal husbandry, inspiration, learning, poetry, prophecy, smithcraft, love.

Patroness of Ireland and dairy workers.

◄ SAINT CLARE OF ASSISI

Feast Day: August 11
Day of the week: Monday
Emblem: A monstrance
Color of candle: White

Petition her aid for the development of understanding, help in difficulties, protection against the evils of body and soul, to overcome drug or alcohol problems.

Patroness of television.

SAINT CATHERINE OF ALEXANDRIA ➤

Feast Day: November 25
Day of the week: Saturday
Emblem: A wheel
Color of candle: Yellow or
     white

Petition her concerning
beauty, fertility, a happy
death, love, femininity,
coquetry, jealousy, healing
and health, lucky birth,
visions and dreams, public
speaking.

Patroness of jurors, philoso-
phers, teachers, wheel-
wrights. Her emblem in art is
the wheel, possibly equating
her with Arianrhod.

SAINT DYMPHNA

Feast Day: May 15
Day of the week: Monday
Emblem: A sword pointed
     down, or a book with a
     shamrock and crest
Color of candle: Blue

Petition in cases of insanity,
obsession with demons,
nervous disorders, mental
afflictions, family harmony,
epilepsy.

SAINT CECILIA ➤

Feast Day: November 22
Day of the week: Wednesday
Emblem: An organ
Color of candle: Green

Petiton her for success in the careers listed below.

Patroness of composers, musicians, organmakers, poets, singers, vocalists.

SAINT FRANCIS XAVIER CABRINI

Feast Day: November 13
Day of the week: Sunday
Color of candle: White

Petition concerning the poor and needy, to be accepted when you have to relocate to another city or state, matters of health, education.

Patroness of all emigrants.

SAINT HELEN OF JERUSALEM

Feast Day: August 18
Day of the week: Friday
Emblem: A cross
Color of candle: Pink or red

Petition to obtain love or the return of a strayed lover, to overcome sorrow and sadness.

Patroness of archaeologists.

SAINT JOAN OF ARC >

Feast day: May 30
Day of the week: Tuesday
Emblem: A suit of armour
Color of candle: Gray

Petition to overcome enemies, for courage, spiritual strength, freedom from confining situations.

Patroness of France.

< SAINT LUCY

Feast day: December 13
Day of the week: Wednesday
Emblem: Two eyes in a dish
Color of candle: White

Petition for eye problems, to keep legal problems away, when life has you down or against a wall, to conquer temptations, protection from the evil eye, to pressure your lawyer to settle your case.

Patroness of peasants, peddlers, saddlers, salesmen.

Saint Martha ➤

Feast day: July 29
Day of the week: Tuesday
Emblem: A dragon
Color of candle: Green and white

Petition for necessities, money problems, domestic problems, to bring closer a lover who is resisting you, to help keep a husband or boyfriend faithful, bring a new love, to conquer and subdue enemies.

Patroness of dieticians, domestic servants, house-keepers, a happy home, innkeepers.

Saint Philomena

Feast day: August 11
Day of the week: Saturday
Emblem: An anchor
Color of candle: Pink or green

For priests and their work, conversion of wrong-doers, return to the Sacraments, expectant mothers, destitute mothers, problems with children, unhappiness in the home, sterility, the sick, real estate, money problems, food for the poor, mental illness.

Patroness of desperate situations, powerful with God.

SAINT RITA OF CASCIA ➤

Feast day: May 22
Day of the week: Sunday
Emblem: A wound on the
    forehead
Color of candle: White

Petition to relieve loneliness,
if in abusive relationships,
for healing wounds, tumors,
for spiritual strength, deliverance from evil, patience.

Patroness of hopeless or
impossible cases.

≺ SAINT THERESE OF LISIEUX

Feast day: October 1
Day of the week: Wednesday
Emblem: A bouquet of roses
Color of candle: Yellow

Petition her for problems
with alcoholism and drugs,
to be loved by all, for
spiritual growth, protection
from harm by enemies
through black magick, to
restore faith, or if afflicted
with tuberculosis.

THE MALE SAINTS

SAINT ANTHONY OF PADUA ➤

Feast Day: June 13
Day of the week: Tuesday
Emblem: A lily
Color of candle: Brown (for special requests), green (for financial needs), orange (for marriage)

Petition for special requests, to find lost articles, improve the memory, for marriage or love problems, to bring back a strayed lover, overcome financial problems.

Patron of lost articles, said to be a wonder-worker.

SAINT ALPHONSUS LIGUORI

Feast day: August 1
Day of the week: Thursday
Color of candle: Purple

Petition in cases of rheumatic fever and disease, arthritis, gout, ailments that affect the joints and muscles, and osteoarthritis.

SAINT ALOYSIUS ➢

Feast day: June 21
Day of the week: Wednesday
Color of candle: Blue

Invoke for cases of fevers, epidemics and plagues, to settle disputes.

➣ SAINT BARTHOLOMEW

Feast Day: August 24
Day of the week: Tuesday
Emblem: A butcher knife
Color of candle: Red

Petition his aid in cases concerning learning the truth, for protection from violence and a violent death, when undergoing surgery.

Patron of butchers, plasterers, surgeons.

SAINT BENEDICT ➤

Feast day: July 11
Day of the week: Saturday
Emblem: A raven and a
broken cup
Color of candle: White

Petition for ending fevers, kidney diseases, against poisons, against evil temptations, for increasing faith, protection against contagious diseases, for a prosperous business, for expectant mothers' safe delivery, during storms, dangers from land or sea, healing of sick animals, assistance at the time of death. Wearing the Jubilee Medal of St. Benedict is recommended.

Patron of monastics, monks, poisonings, speleologists.

SAINT ALEX/SAINT ALEXIS/ SAN ALEJO

Feast Day: July 17
Day of the week: Sunday
Emblem: A crucifix
Color of candle: Pink

He is petitioned to keep your enemies away, for protection from the harm your enemies wish for you.

Patron of beggars, beltmakers, nursing society called Alexian Brothers.

SAINT BLAISE/BLAS ➤

Feast day: February 3
Day of the week: Wednesday
Emblem: Comb or two
     crossed candles
Color of candle: Blue

Petition concerning diseases in humans and animals, disease and infections of the throat, to open the lines of communication with others.

Patron of the throat and wild animals.

In the Catholic ceremony honoring the feast day of St. Blaise, all who desired a blessing of their throat came before the priest. He placed a pair of crossed candles to the person's throat, pronouncing a blessing on the throat. In magico-religious thinking, the action clearly illustrates the spirit of St. Blase being channeled through the body of the priest; using his symbol, the two crossed candles.

SAINT FLORIAN

Feast day: May 4
Day of the week: Sunday
Emblem: A burning house
Color of candle: Red or
     orange

Petition to protect the home from fire, protection when in danger, and for help in emergencies.

Saint Florian is a patron of firemen.

Saint Christopher ➤

Feast day: July 25
Day of the week: Wednesday
Color of candle: Red

Petition for cases against impenitence at death, for protection from accidents, against sudden death, safe travel, to cure contagious fevers, against hail, storms.

Patron of bachelors, bus drivers, hazards of traveling, motorists, porters.

Saints Cosmas and Damian

Feast day: September 27
Day of the week: Wednesday
Emblem: Herbs and palm
Color of candle: Green (2)

Petition for health matters, sickness, correct diagnosis and medication, to fight for your behalf, against obstacles.

Patron of barbers, chemical industries, druggists, physicians, surgeons.

Saint Cipriano

Feast day: October 9
Day of the week: Saturday
Color of candle: Purple

It is said that this saint was raised in black magick before converting to Christianity. Invoked for help when traveling, to protect from harm, from bad language, and from jails, for homeless people, protection from lightning, thunder, fire, and earthquakes, from bad neighbors harassing you, liars and cheaters of the heart.

SAINT EXPEDITE ➤

Feast day: April 19
Day of the week: Thursday
Emblem: A raven and cross
    with the letters HODIE
Color of candle: Yellow

Petition for settling disputes,
to work death curses on
your enemy, and for pressing
cases where things need to
change quickly.

SAINT GERARD MAJELLA

Feast day: October 16
Day of the week: Monday
Emblem: A crucifix and a lily
Color of candle: White

Petition to become pregnant,
for expectant mothers,
mothers with small children,
when falsely accused, for
ecstasies, channeling, medi-
umship, prophecy, the ability
to read consciences, healing,
to see the truth.

Patron of expectant mothers.

SAINT FRANCIS OF ASSISI ➤

Feast day: October 4
Day of the week: Monday
Emblem: Stigmata
Color of candle: Brown

Petition for better understanding, peace, to detect evil plots, to gain spiritual wisdom, help with problems, in matters of ecology and conservation.

Patron of animals, birds, Catholic action, firemen, lace workers, merchants, needle workers, a solitary death.

◄ SAINT GEORGE

Feast day: April 23
Day of the week: Tuesday
Emblem: A shield with a red cross on white, a dragon
Color of candle: Red

Petition to conquer fear, for courage, to overcome jealousy, dry skin, eczema, mental retardation, sores.

Patron of soldiers, Boy Scouts, Cavalry, England.

SAINT IGNATIUS OF LOYOLA ➤

Feast Day: July 31
Day of the week: Saturday
Emblem: A book and a plum
Color of candle: White

Petition to protect the house from burglars and evil spirits, for spiritual development.

Patron of the Jesuit Order, spiritual retreats, soldiers.

SAINT JAMES THE GREATER

Feast day: July 25
Day of the week: Tuesday
Emblem: Cockleshell
Color of candle: Red

Petition to conquer your enemies, to clear away obstacles in your path, for justice.

Patron of manual laborers, rheumatism, Spain.

SAINT JOACHIM

Feast Day: July 26
Day of the week: Friday
Emblem: Two doves in a basket
Color of candle: Green

Petition for a faithful husband.

SAINT JOHN THE BAPTIST ≻

Feast day: June 24
Day of the week: Tuesday
Color of candle: Green

Petition for good luck, good crops, fertility, protection from enemies.

Patron of conversion and baptism, tailors.

≺ SAINT JOHN BOSCO

Feast day: January 31
Day of the week: Sunday
Color of candle: Yellow

Petition for favors, temporal needs, problems with children, students.

Patron of editors, the Salesians Missionary Order.

SAINT JOSEPH ≻

Feast day: March 19
Day of the week: Sunday
Emblem: Lily
Color of candle: Yellow

Petition for protection, a happy death, to find a job, sell a home, to end famine, in cases of doubt and hesitation, for married couples.

Patron of Belgium, Canada, carpenters, confectioners, Peru, pioneers, the Universal Church.

SAINT JOSEPH THE WORKER

Feast Day: May 1
Day of the week: Wednesday
Emblem: a pitcher and a loaf
   of bread

Petition for the same as Saint Joseph.

SAINT LAWRENCE

Feast day: August 10
Day of the week: Wednesday
Emblem: A gridiron
Color of candle: Red

Petition for a peaceful home and family, for financial assistance, increased faith.

Patron of Ceylon and the poor.

Saint Jude ➣

Feast day: October 28
Day of the week: Sunday
Emblem: A medal and a staff
Color of candle: Green, white,
 and red

Petition for hopeless or
impossible cases, to help
someone get off drugs, to
help someone get out of jail.

≺ Saint Lazarus

Feast day: December 17
Day of the week: Sunday
Emblem: A pair of crutches
 and two dogs
Color of candle: Yellow

Petition for the sick, infirmi-
ties of the legs, for problems
with drug addictions, to
maintain health, for obtaining prosperity.

Patron saint of smallpox.

Saint Martin de Porres >

Feast day: November 3
Day of the week: Thursday
Emblem: Broom and crucifix
Color of candle: Purple and
   white

Petition for financial needs,
health, to bring harmony.

Patron of Afro-Americans,
poor and needy, animals.

< Saint Martin of Tours (Saint Martin Caballero)

Feast day: November 11
Day of the week: Tuesday
Emblem: Sword, torn cape
Color of candle: Red or white

Petition to block the path
of evil, protection from
enemies, to rescue someone
from evil influences, draw
customers to your business,
money, luck, prosperity.

SAINT PATRICK ➤

Feast day: March 17
Day of the week: Sunday
Emblem: Shamrock and
   snakes
Color of candle: White

Petition for protection
against snakebite, prosperity,
luck, spiritual wisdom,
guidance.

Patron of Ireland.

◄ SAINT PAUL

Feast Day: June 29
Day of the week: Tuesday
Emblem: A sword and a book
Color of candle: Blue or red

Petition for courage, to overcome opposition, develop
patience, to settle disturbed
conditions in the home.

Patron of authors, journal-
ists, the press, publishers,
travel, writers.

SAINT PETER ➤

Feast day: June 29
Day of week: Tuesday
Emblem: Two crossed keys
Color of candle: Red and
   white

Petition for success, remove
obstacles, better business,
strength and courage, forgiveness of hurts, good luck
(fortune).

Patron of bridge builders,
clock makers, fever, foot
trouble, frenzy, long life,
masons, net makers, ship
builders, stationers, wolves.

SAINT PEREGRINE

Feast day: May 1 or 2
Day of the week: Sunday
Emblem: Shepherd's crook
   with purse tied to it
Color of candle: White

Petition for health problems
involving cancer.

SAINT PIUS THE TENTH

Feast day: August 21
Day of the week: Sunday
Color of candle: White

Petition for special requests,
for favors granted from those
in authority.

Patron of first communicants.

SAINT RAYMOND NONNATUS ➤

Feast day: August 31
Day of the week: Tuesday
Emblem: Monstrance and
   palm with three crowns
Color of candle: Red

Petition for stopping gossip,
when falsely accused, protection of unborn babies, for a
blessed home.

Patron of midwives.

SAINT LOUIS BERTRAND (SAINT LOUIS BELTRAN)

Feast day: October 9
Emblem: A crucifix attached
   to a tongue
Color of candle: White

Petition for learning lan-
guages, protection from evil,
accidents, sickness, and
harm from enemies, invoke
to remove the malochia from
children.

SAINT ROCH OR ROQUE (ALSO SPELLED ROCK)

Feast day: August 16
Day of the week: Wednesday
Emblem: Dog
Color of candle: Yellow

Petition to restore health,
during times of plague or
yellow fever.

Patron of dog fanciers.

SAINT SEBASTIAN ➤

Feast day: January 20
Day of the week: Tuesday
Emblem: Arrows
Color of candle: Red

Petition for justice, court cases, to overcome rivals, remove obstacles, success, good fortune.

Patron of archers, armorers, arrowsmiths, athletes, cattle diseases, enemies of religion, gardeners, bookbinders, hardware, iron mongers, lead workers, potters, racquet makers, soldiers, stone masons, undertakers.

≺ SAINT THOMAS AQUINAS

Feast day: January 28
Day of the week: Monday
Emblem: a star
Color of candle: White

Petition for understanding, to improve memory, pass school exams.

Patron of scholars, schools, Catholic universities, pencil makers, students, and theologians.

THE ANGELIC SAINTS

GUARDIAN ANGEL

Day of the week: Monday
Color of candle: White

Petition for protection of
children, against the evil eye,
to gain spiritual strength
during difficult times, guidance in daily affairs.

SAINT RAPHAEL
THE ARCHANGEL

Feast day: September 29
Color of candle: Pink

Petition for a safe journey, to
be reunited with loved ones,
to cure all sickness, to cut
away evil spirits, to protect
from possession by spirits, in
times of need.

Patron of apothecaries,
druggists, eye diseases,
lovers, nurses, physicians,
sheep raisers.

SAINT MICHAEL
THE ARCHANGEL ➤

Feast day: September 29
Color of candle: Red, purple,
   and green

Petition for deliverance from
enemies, protection from evil
and harm, victory in battle,
protection of home and
business, to protect from
police harassment.

Patron of Germany, grocers,
knights, paratroopers,
peril at sea, policemen,
radiologists, seafarers.

CHAPTER 2

DIVINATION IN MAGICO RELIGIOUS PRACTICE

D ivination in any form is invariably condemned by fundamental Christians, who are quick to point out such scriptures as Acts 16:16–18:

"As we were going to the place of prayer, we met a slave girl with an oracular spirit, who used to bring a large profit to her owners through her fortunetelling. She began to follow Paul and us, shouting, 'These people are slaves of the Most High God, who proclaim to you a way of salvation.' She did this for many days. Paul became annoyed, turned, and said to the spirit, 'I command you in the name of Jesus Christ to come out of her.' Then it came out at that moment."

The scripture above and all other scripture quoted in this book is taken from the Saint Joseph Edition of the New American Bible. Footnotes in this bible interpret the meaning of certain words or phrases. For the phrase "with an oracular spirit" the footnotes explain "literally, 'with a Python spirit.' The Python was the serpent or dragon that guarded the Delphic oracle. It later came to designate a 'spirit that pronounces oracles' and also a ventriloquist who, it was thought, had 'such a spirit in the belly.'" This seems to be a rude definition of channeling; or as Christians would call it, "falling out in the spirit," "passing the spirit," or "filled with the spirit."

Fundamentalists would tell you that St. Paul cast out an evil spirit or devil from the slave girl with an oracular spirit. In fact, the passages themselves do not prove the belief that the spirit channeled through the girl is evil. Verse 18 provides the reason Paul cast out the spirit. He was annoyed by the spirit, because it was proclaiming a truth about him.

Though the reason was not given, Paul did not want too many people to know about him at that period of time. It was the truth that annoyed him, not the spirit.

Fundamentalist Christians point out other verses such as Leviticus 19:26: "Do not practice divination or soothsaying." Also in Leviticus verse 31: "Do not go to mediums or consult fortune-tellers." Now, these same Fundamentalists are unlikely to bring to your attention biblical verses that seem to prove that the Christian God the Father allowed certain forms of divination to be practiced and did, indeed, establish a form of divination among his own priesthood.

Genesis 44:4–5 relates: "They had not gone far out of the city when Joseph said to his head steward: 'Go at once after the men! When you overtake them, say to them, 'Why did you repay good with evil? Why did you steal the silver goblet from me?'

"'It is the very one from which my master drinks and which he uses for divination. What you have done is wrong.'"

The footnote to 44:5 explains: "Divination: seeking omens through liquids poured into a cup or bowl was a common practice in the ancient Near East." Even though in Israel divination was frowned on later (Lv 19:31), it is in this place an authentic touch which the sacred author does not hesitate to ascribe to Joseph, who was considered to be the wisest man in Egypt.

In verse 15 of the same chapter we read: "'How could you do such a thing?' Joseph asked them. 'You should have known that such a man as I could discover by divination what happened.'" The technique of divination used here is called scrying. Chapters 40 and 41 of Genesis deal with Joseph interpreting the dreams of Pharaoh as well as the dreams of others. Other verses point out that God does speak to humans through dreams:

Here we have two kinds of divination: scrying and interpretation of dreams. Scrying literally means to see the future or the past and the present. The visions seen during a scrying session do not literally appear within the medium used as a focal point, but will appear within your peripheral vision. Initially, in learning to scry, you will want to work alone in a room that is quiet so that you are not disturbed. However, the room should be dark, using one or two candles as the only source of light. It is extremely important that the light does not reflect upon the surface of the crystal ball or mirror you are using as a focal point of concentration as this can interfere with the formation of the visions received. For more on this subject, see *Scrying for Beginners: Tapping Into the Supersensory*

Powers of Your Subconscious by Donald Tyson (St. Paul: Llewellyn Publications, 1997).

Chapter 20:3: "But God came to Abimelech in a dream one night and said to him...." Chapter 31:11: "In the dream God's messenger called to me, 'Jacob!'"

In verse 19 we read, "Now Laban had gone away to shear his sheep, and Rachel had meanwhile appropriated her father's household idols." The footnote reads: "Genesis 31:19: Household idols: in Hebrew, terrapin, figurines used in divination."

Ezekiel 21:26: "For at the fork where the two roads divide stands the king of Babylon, divining; he has shaken the arrows, inquired of the seraphim, inspected the liver."

Here the footnote reads: "Three forms of divination are mentioned: arrow divination, which consisted in the use of differently marked arrows extracted or shaken from a case at random; the consultation of the teraphim or household idols; and liver divination, which was the careful study of the livers of newly slaughtered animals, a common practice of divination in Mesopatamia." In Genesis 31:30 Laban calls the teraphim his "gods." We read: "Granted that you had to leave because you were desperately homesick for your father's house, why did you steal my gods?" Going back to verse 24 of chapter 31, God speaks through a dream for we read: "But that night God appeared to Laban the Aramean in a dream and warned him."

In the second book of the bible, Exodus, God established a system of divination among his own priesthood. "The breastpiece of decision you shall have made, embroidered like the ephod with gold thread and violet" (Exodus 28:15). Skipping down to verse 30 we read: "In this breastpiece of decision you shall put the Urim and Thummim, that they may be over Aaron's heart whenever he enters the presence of the Lord." All Hebrew words ending in 'im' are plural words by nature of the language. The footnote regarding the Urim and Thummim states that both the meaning of the words and exact nature of the objects used are uncertain. They were apparently lots of some sort that were drawn or cast to ascertain God's decision in doubtful matters.

In Leviticus chapter 16:7–8 we read how the Urim and Thummim were used by the Priest. "Taking the two male goats, and setting them before the Lord at the entrance of the meeting tent, he (the Priest) shall cast lots to determine which one is for the Lord and which one is for Azazel."

Chapter 33, verse 8 of Deuteronomy gives us a clue about the lots: "To Levi belong your Thummim, to the man of your favor your Urim." This seems to suggest that the Thummim gave a negative or a no answer, whereas the Urim gave a positive or a yes answer to a question. Another point that illustrates the Hebrew God of the Old Testament speaking through a form of divination is in Numbers 27:2: "He shall present himself to the priest Eleazar, to have him seek out for him the decisions of the Urim in the Lord's presence." The New International Version of the Holy Bible interprets this verse as: "He is to stand before Eleazar the Priest, who will obtain decisions for him by inquiring of the Urim before the Lord!" Again the footnote to this passage refers to the Urim as a certain sacred object which the Hebrew priests employed to ascertain the divine will, probably by obtaining a positive or negative answer to a question.

Again in scripture we read that divination is a function of the priesthood. It is written in Ezra 2:62–63: "These men searched the family records, but their names could not be found written there; hence they were degraded from the priesthood, and His Excellency ordered them not to partake of the most holy foods until there should be a priest bearing the Urim and Thummim." These same two verses in Ezra are repeated in Nehemiah, 7:64–65. It is revealed in Numbers 12:6 that God will not verbally speak to men as he spoke with Moses but will use other means, for it is written:, "Now listen to the words of the Lord: Should there be a prophet among, you, in visions will I reveal myself to him, in dreams will I speak to him," and verse 7 reads: "Not so with my servant Moses!" It is already established that God used the Urim and Thummim to speak through his priesthood instead of verbally as he did with Moses. And lastly, an old testament scripture pointing out that God permits the practice of divination appears in Deuteronomy 13:2–4: "If there arises among you a prophet or a dreamer who promises you a sign or wonder, urging you to follow other gods, whom you have not known, and to serve them: even though the sign or wonder he has foretold has come to pass, pay no attention to the words of that prophet or that dreamer; for the Lord your God is testing you to learn whether you really love him with all your heart and with all your soul."

The admonition here is not against the practice [of] divination in its diverse forms, but against seeking out the deities of a different culture and religion. The words of the admonition are clearly underlined.

The point of all of this is to illustrate to New Age teaching and religion a basic truth about psychic abilities such as clairvoyance, clairaudience, and other forms of divination in general, that psychic ability is *not a gift from God*, as most people commonly believe, *nor is it a power from the devil or Satan,* as Christian ministers want the public to believe. It is a natural ability inherent in human beings, a skill that can be developed through disciplined spiritual training, which does not occur overnight. In many societies young men and women displaying some form of natural psychic ability were automatically trained to join the ranks of the societies' religious leaders. In most instances it took years of training to learn the system of divination used by a particular culture. These young men and women underwent a rigorous, disciplined training employing spiritual exercises to develop their natural psychic ability. It is an easy task to memorize the meanings to forty-eight, fifty-two, or seventy-eight cards, but without investing the time to develop psychic ability by diligently practicing spiritual exercises to aid the growth and development of this wonderful natural ability, your readings will come to nothing. Your reading will not be of a genuine nature that will really help anyone, but will be merely a form of entertainment to pass the time. Memorizing the meanings of cards does not automatically give a person genuine psychic ability.

Divination is the beginning to all rituals in magico-religious practice. All the ingredients that are necessary to help solve a person's problem can be determined exactly through divination. It is through divination that a particular offering given to a saint, spirit, or deity will be accepted or not. Within a magico-religious practice there is an element of guarantee. There is no reason for the petitioner to feel that his or her request will not be granted if the instructions given during the divination session are followed.

In all references in the Holy Bible of divination practiced by Jehovah's priesthood, an object of some sort was used as a focal point of concentration, except in the Book of Acts where it is written that the slave girl had an oracular spirit. This form of divination could be called *theomancy*, meaning divination by oracles, and by persons inspired by God. New Age thinking would refer to this as channeling. The very first form of divination mentioned in scripture is called *oneiromancy*, meaning by dreams. A third type of divination, commonly called scrying, Joseph practiced using a goblet filled with liquid. This ancient method is still practiced today, using as focal points of concentration objects such as a crystal ball, a quartz crystal, or a magic or black mirror.

Another instance of divination involves the use of figurines, called household idols; in Hebrew, *teraphim*. The closest thing that compares with this is the use of *igbos*, associated with Santerian seashell divination. Sixteen cowrie shells are used in this type of divination, along with these figures or igbos: a tiny doll or a doll's head, a long, oval-shaped seashell, a small black stone, a piece of bone, and finally a piece of cascarilla. This technique is a fine example of magico-religious divination. It is a system that can take fifteen years of study to master, ending with a ceremony of initiation into the priesthood.

A lesser-known form of divination, *belomancy,* is divination by arrows. This is followed by *hepatoscopy,* divining by reading the livers of animals. When Jehovah or Yaweh instructed his priesthood to use the Urim and Thummim, they were practicing a divination technique called *sortilege.* Sortilege is divination by lots. It is a common belief that the Urim and Thummim were lots of some sort, cast to determine divine will. This technique also includes *rhabdomancy* (divination with the aid of a divining rod, staff, or wand), belomancy, and similar procedures. Sortilege is the technique mentioned more than any other method in biblical scripture.

Since the invention of tarot cards and emergence of playing cards, cartomancy has become a very popular form of divination. Some cultures combine cartomancy and sortilege in one system. This method of magico-religious divination is used in the islands of the Gulf of Mexico as well as by some people in Louisiana. Modern-day objects commonly used in the practice of sortilege are: four cowrie shells, sixteen cowrie shells combined with the igbos, rune casting, four pieces of coconut, or four pieces of kola nut, and the Druid sticks, described by Richard Webster in *Omens, Oghams & Oracles* (Llewellyn Publications, 1995). The *fidlanna* is taught by Kisma K. Stepanich in her book *Faery Wicca: Book Two* (Llewellyn, 1995). She refers to the fidlanna as faery lots.

Most people would refer to Druid sticks as *geomancy.* Geomancy is divination by an examination of handfuls of earth, by dots on paper, or marks made on the earth. Whether you call the Druid sticks geomancy or sortilege is not important. Both are interpreted according to a set pattern of sixteen combinations.

Another method of divination, though not mentioned in the scriptures referred to earlier, is *xylomancy,* which means divination by sticks. Rhabdomancy is written of in Hosea 4:12: "They consult their piece of wood, and their wand makes pronouncements for them," and in the New International Version of the Holy Bible this verse is written as: "They consult a wooden idol and are answered by a stick of wood." This technique, known and written of during biblical times, is taught today as the Saxon Wands by Raymond Buckland in his *Buckland's Complete Book of Witchcraft* (Llewellyn Publications, 1986). Also see Buckland's *Secrets of Gypsy Fortunetelling* (Llewellyn, 1995) and *The Tree: Complete Book of Saxon Witchcraft* (Samuel Weiser, 1995). Another modern-day example is the Bodhran Drum divination in Webster's *Omens, Oghams & Oracles* (1995). These systems are similar to the I-Ching, but they are more direct and straightforward in the interpretation of each pattern.

In magico-religious practice, it is the Diviner Priest or Priestess who keeps the community in close contact with the culture's concept of Divinity. All rituals are begun with divination as a safeguard to prevent a mistake from being made. Diviner Priests or Priestesses are introduced through rites of initiation/ordination after two to three years of study, participation in group rituals, and practicing spiritual exercises. Gemstones and crystals are used to balance the psychic centers, and incense is used to fumigate the spiritual bodies. Fumigation aids in removing negative energy attaching itself to the aura, which a spiritual bath alone will not remove. The fumigation raises the energy passing through the body to a higher level, similar to the Amerindian practice of smudging to remove negativity and cleanse the spiritual body.

In my own ordination ceremony, at one point the initiating priest chanted prayers as he sacrificed live animals above my head. Though my eyes were closed, I could feel the warmth and wetness of the blood falling on my head. The seal was set. After the ceremony I was required to wear only white for nine days and cover my head with a white cap when I went outdoors. The initiation/ordination to become a Diviner Priest or Priestess guarantees that one will never give a cold reading. As you begin to study the system of divination used, you are taught the prayers to open the divination session and the procedure to close it.

In my own method of divination I combine cartomancy and sortilege, the technique I was taught by a Voodoo priest. He taught me how to read the cowrie shell I use and how to combine the shell reading with the cartomancy I already knew. In reality, a Diviner Priest or Priestess can give a complete investigative reading into a problem by using one of the tools of sortilege alone. In practice, I reveal what the cards are saying as I listen to the client and confirm the reading through sortilege. This method will help you diagnose the number of candles needed and their color, according to the client's situation or problem: what prayers the client should be using; if a spiritual bath is needed, and if a "yes" answer is given, will it require herbs in light composition? If you get a "yes" answer, you will then need to ask what type or types of herbs. All herbs used must pertain to the nature of the problem. Will the client benefit from having a gris-gris/mojo made? If so, then what ingredients should be used to make it? Will you need to perform a folk spell to aid the client in getting the problem solved? A Diviner Priest or Priestess has to have a working knowledge of natural and sympathetic magic, and know the magical properties of the herbs, stones, or whatever else may be used. This knowledge should be firmly set in their minds in order for them to work effectively.

Through sortilege you can diagnose if the client is blessed with good luck in spite of the problem; the source of their bad luck; if they are being hexed deliberately by another's use of a spell or the evil eye; or if the client is actually hexing themselves by not using their heads or through carelessness. At times a hexed condition is caused by gossip alone.

To protect yourself, you must always ask first if you have permission to involve yourself with the problem of another person by composing a mojo or doing a spell. If the answer is "NO," then all the work that is needed is for the client to burn a candle setup with prayers. If a spiritual bath is needed it can be made by the client. All you need to do is give the client complete instructions and the prayers that should be said. If a bath is prescribed by sortilege, then you need to determine if the bath needs to be taken X number of days consecutively, or if it needs to be taken on certain days of the week and for a certain period of time. At times a client may need to wear charged oil or cologne that has certain herbs added to it. This the client can prepare for him- or herself.

A wonderful kit currently on the market is *The Book of African Divination* by Raymond Buckland and Kathleen Binger (U.S. Games, 1997). It draws upon diverse African traditions of magical divination practices, from Venda tablets to Zulu bone casting (sortilege) and Tiker spider cards.

SPIRITUAL BATHS

In the New Orleans area, practitioners make the spiritual baths for their clients. Sometimes a poor client will pay $25 or more for a gallon mixture. The practitioner will instruct the client to use one-third of the gallon per bath. The client will be told that they will need to take, for example, nine baths. The practitioner will prepare three one-gallon containers of the bath mixture and collect $75 or more from the client. In this case the client is being defrauded. More than one practitioner has told me straight out: *always* sell your client a spiritual bath, whether they need it or not, because it will not hurt them, and you will collect more money from the client than he or she was planning to spend. Here is one example where clients are deliberately being defrauded. The reality is that one cup of the gallon mixture is sufficient for one spiritual bath; thus one gallon will yield sixteen spiritual baths.

Beware! You will have a few clients who will act very desperate, portraying themselves as innocent victims wanting something done against another. They will deliberately lie to you as they relate their story. You will have a few clients knowing full well that they are guilty of doing wrong to another, and who are making a desperate attempt to escape the consequences of their own actions. In reality, the other person to whom the client wants something evil done is completely innocent of wrongdoing toward the client. In almost all cases these people will swear that they are good church-going Christians. Then it becomes the task of the Diviner Priest or Priestess to aid the client in such a way as to allow Universal Law to decide who is the guilty party in the situation. Aiding a client to take revenge on another will cause that client to pay the price of bad luck somewhere down the line. We all reap what we sow.

Divination within magico-religious practice is not necessarily the same type of reading you would get from a psychic reader or a psychic phone line. Most psychics do not give negative readings because this is what they learn from books and are taught by other psychics. This practice of not giving a negative reading ignores reality. A Diviner Priest or Priestess *will* give a negative reading to a client. For example: a woman came to me because her daughter was in trouble. The daughter had been arrested and was in jail in Mississippi charged with writing checks amounting to $2,500 on insufficient funds. She was going to trial the following month. The mother wanted something done to get her daughter out of the problem smelling like a rose, because just prior to the arrest her daughter had started going back to church. The reading was negative. The daughter would spend time in prison to pay the price of her actions, because she knew that she did not have the money in the bank to cover the checks when she wrote them. The only chance that the daughter could escape a prison sentence was if the mother herself was able to pay the $2,500, plus court costs. Naturally this would have put the woman's mother in a financial situation she could not afford. Here a client is being unrealistic about the situation. Another example is a female client who came to me because she was lonely and wanted a man in her life. The woman was doing the work prescribed to help find a companion, but she was unwilling to change her pattern of living. Her pattern was: work and home, work and home. Naturally she was not getting results because she did not want to put herself in a situation where she could meet new people. At the next reading I had to tell her straight out, "If you are not willing to change this pattern, forget about finding a companion, because *Jesus is not coming down from heaven,* knocking on your door to introduce you to anyone."

Then she said, "I thought that prayer changed things."

Yes, prayer can change things, provided that you do your part to obtain your desires. It is sad when people are encouraged by overzealous spiritual leaders to think that all they have to do is ask in Jesus' name and it will be given to them, while they sit back and do nothing.

On the other hand, I had a case in which a mother came to me in desperation with her seventeen-year-old son. The son had to go to court in two or three weeks on five counts of breaking the law: three counts for possession and selling of drugs, and two counts of resisting arrest. The mother did not have a lawyer to defend her son. Through divination I diagnosed that a blue candle and a purple candle needed to be kept burning until the trial date. I had to prepare a gris-gris/mojo to win a court case, make the spiritual bath myself, and spiritually cleanse the boy's aura using fresh herbs, colognes, holy water, incense, and fire. When everything was completed, I said to the boy, "It is important that you say the truth in court. By saying the truth you will escape a jail sentence." A few days after the trial the mother and her son came back to thank me because, just prior to the case coming before the judge, a lawyer appeared to represent her son. Three of the five charges were dropped. The boy was put on one year of supervised probation and one year of unsupervised probation. After telling me all this, the boy happily said, "I never knew that my mama loved me so much until she had to turn to voodoo to get me out of my trouble." The divination session was a success because the boy was spared prison time, but he still had to pay for his actions through serving the probation time.

And so I leave you with a few verses from Acts 2:23–36:

"So they proposed two, Joseph called Barsabbas, who was also known as Justus, and Matthias. Then they prayed, 'You, Lord, who knows the hearts of all, show which one of these two you have chosen to take the place in this apostolic ministry from which Judas turned away to go on his own place.' Then they gave lots to them, and the lot fell upon Matthias and he was counted with the eleven apostles."

The successor of Judas was chosen through a system of divination. Fundamentalist Christians will deny this statement, and will point out other scriptures condemning all practices of divination, ignoring the scriptures proving that Jehovah instructed his priesthood in divination. All of Jehovah's priests came from the tribe of Levi. If a person did not belong to this tribe it was not possible for him to become a member of the priesthood. Laws were written down to prevent anyone from using divination who was not of the priesthood, even if the person did in fact have genuine psychic ability. Think about it: the ancient Hebrew religion was probably modeled after the

Egyptian form of government, in which the priesthood was actually in charge behind the scenes, with Pharoah in the foreground. I firmly believe in the separation of church and state. Religious leaders have consistently sought control over the population through instilling fear and superstition in the minds of the people. They still do so today, just as an unscrupulous diviner will use a form of divination to instill fear and superstition in conning a client out of as much money as they can get their hands on. A genuine, sincere, and honest diviner priest or priestess will never be ashamed to use his or her real name. If they have the title of reverend or bishop before their name and you do not see in the consultation room a certificate of ordination from a validly registered church, then the title is a lie.

CHAPTER 3

HONORING THE ANCESTORS
AND THE DEAD

T his may be labeled by many as ancestor worship and condemned by Fundamentalist Christians, but Roman Catholic teaching says: "Although the souls in purgatory cannot merit, they are able to pray and obtain the fruit of prayer. The power of their prayers depends on their sanctity. It is certain that they can pray and obtain blessings for those living on earth. They are united with the pilgrim Church in the Communion of Saints." Printed instructions for novenas and prayers for the dead can be found at any Catholic religious supply house. I was raised using the novena written by St. Alphonsus de Liguori, which contained a different prayer for each of the nine days of the novena, plus a rosary for the dead and another set of general prayers for each weekday. In the second book of Maccabees, chapter 12:42–46, we read about the ancient Jewish custom of offering prayers and sacrifices on behalf of the dead. This custom is still carried over into some Christian teaching, but frowned upon by most Protestant Christians. The first and second books of Maccabees were removed by King James from his authorized version of the Holy Bible—the version which most Protestants today read.

For close to ninety percent of the world's population, ritual offerings and prayers to defunct blood relatives form an integral part of everyday living. The practice is universal in nature, common to people raised in Eastern cultures such as the Chinese, Koreans, Japanese, and Tibetans, as well as large segments of South America, Mexico, Cuba, Haiti, in the indigenous religions of Africa, Bali, Indonesia, Polynesia, Mongolia, spreading into Europe in the Baltic States and Iceland, as well as among the ancient Celtic peoples whose modern descendants still carry on customs associated with the dead to this very day.

Honoring the ancestors can provide you with knowledge that all of life is a continuum, and enable you to actually communicate with the energy of your departed family members. Any form of communicating with the dead is called *necromancy*. The practice of necromancy does involve conjuring up the spirit of a defunct personage to obtain information about a future event. This is often pointed out in 1 Samuel 28:7–25, when King Saul consulted the woman of Endor. Biblical scripture calls this woman a witch, but in reality she was a necromancer, revealed in verse 11 when she asks King Saul, "Whom do you want me to conjure up?" There is not a genuine witch that I personally know of who practices this sort of communication with the dead. The footnote in my Catholic Bible states clearly that human beings cannot communicate at will with the souls of the departed. God may permit a departed soul to appear to the living and even to disclose things unknown to them.

In most instances, the deceased will communicate with their living family members through dreams or ooneiromancy. In my own experience one afternoon I was taking a nap. I dreamed that my mother, two of my brothers, who are currently living, and I went to visit my grandmother. Now my grandmother had been deceased for six years prior to this dream. In the dream, before going to my grandmother's house we stopped at the home of a relative living on the same street for a short visit. My brothers had disappeared, so I set off to look for them, and found them playing in the back yard of our grandmother's home. I noticed that the back door was open, so I went inside to look around. When entering, I saw my grandmother sitting in the living room and I said, "Oh, Grandma you're home."

Then she said to me, "Yes, I've been waiting for you. Where's your mom?"

I said, "She is down the street, visiting Alice. I'll go get her and tell her that you are home."

My grandmother replied, "Fine. I'll cook some ground beef for y'all to eat when you get back, but I want you to play numbers 6, 3, and 7 in the lotto."

There I woke up. Every day I played the numbers given in the dream, except for the following Saturday. I was so busy that day that by the time I was able to purchase my ticket it was too late for the night's lotto drawing. That night the numbers given to me in the dream were drawn. Had I been able to play the numbers, I would have been $500 richer.

New Testament scripture gives a good example of Jesus communicating with the dead. Of course, Protestant ministers and some Catholics will never bring this to your attention. In Matthew 17:1–3; we read:

> After six days Jesus took Peter, James, and John his brother, and led them up a high mountain by themselves. And he was transfigured before them; his face shone like the sun and his cloths became white as light. And behold, Moses and Elijah appeared to them, conversing to him.

From Old Testament scripture we know that Moses had died and was buried, for God knows how many centuries past. It is written in Deuteronomy 34:5: "So there, in the land of Moab, Moses, the servant of the Lord, died as the Lord had said." Therefore it is an accepted practice by God when the dead come of their own free will to communicate with the living. If Jesus, who is supposed to be without sin, did it, then it is permitted by God for others to do so, and yes, the deceased can literally appear before the living, God permitting the dead to communicate with the living as in the case of Moses appearing before Jesus in the sight of Peter, James, and John.

In my own experience, I have seen during a spirit session, as we were praying for the dead, the spirit of a man appear behind the woman sitting opposite from me. As the male spirit put his arm around the woman, she shuddered and made a sound. The woman asked me what I was looking at when she saw me staring, with my mouth open wide. After I described the male spirit who had hugged her, the woman left the room, then came back with two pictures, asking me if one of the men I had described was in either of these two pictures. The picture I verified as the spirit I saw was that of her husband, who had been dead for fifteen years. There was no practice of conjuring up the dead in this form of necromancy, nor in the case when Moses appeared to Jesus.

Conjuring up the dead is not a practice of a diviner priest or priestess. Neither is it a practice of genuine witches practicing their religion today. At Samhain, the eve of November 1, during the religious celebration honoring the departed ancestors, they are not conjured up, but instead they are invited to come forward if they wish to give a message and partake of any offerings of food, flowers, glasses of water, and candies dedicated to their memory. It is commonly believed that on this night the veil between the world of the living and the dead is very thin, making it possible to communicate with the deceased of their own free will. Not our wills. The deceased can communicate with the living at any time they wish.

The technique of sortilege I learned has a pattern that will give a clue that an ancestral spirit may wish to communicate something on behalf of a client's situation. If so, then any answer given through the sortilege afterward will be that of a deceased blood relative speaking. There is no conjuring up the dead involved here because the deceased is coming of their own free will. It may be that the client must take the problem to the ancestors for help in solving the situation. Therefore all prayers and offerings will be dedicated to them. To do this requires almost daily communication with your deceased blood relatives and offerings periodically given to them.

Bridging the gap of communication with the ancestors is really quite simple. To begin you should get a detailed list of all your blood relatives—as complete as possible. You will also need to have the discipline to set aside in the same day at least thirteen minutes of prayer. A white candle is lit for the ancestors, and a clear glass of water set out. Your prayers should go something like this:

Blessings to all my departed ancestors.

I pay my respects to my great, great grandparents (say each name three times).

I pay my respects to my grandparents (say each name three times).

I pay my respects to my great grandparents (say each name three times).

I pay my respects to my great aunt(s) (say each name three times).

I pay my respects to my great uncle(s) (say each name three times).

I pay my respects to my aunt(s) (say each name three times).

I pay my respects to my uncle(s) (say each name three times).

I pay my respects to my deceased father or mother (say their names three times).

Then proceed by saying something like:

> *Accept this cool water that you may have refreshment.*
>
> *Accept this light and energy, so that you may have comfort and strength.*
>
> *Your presence is greatly missed here on earth.*
>
> *Forget not your posterity.*
>
> *May you continue to bring to us your guidance and wisdom, peace in our lives, health and prosperity for our homes.*

Most individuals set a table covered with a white cloth in a corner of the room. On this table are placed as many photographs of their blood relatives as possible. I remember in the early 1960s seeing in people's homes photos of the deceased in their coffins. In fact, an aunt of mine has a painting of my grandmother, Adeline Porche Malbrough, made from a photograph of her in her coffin. In the portrait painting her eyes are closed. This custom has died out recently; it is criticized as a morbid practice. It is permissible for you, yourself, to be in the picture, but not any other living person. To do so could hasten that person's early demise, and you could be held accountable spiritually for murder. Many people place on their ancestral shrine favorite objects associated with the deceased relative. Whatever item you choose must have, in your mind, a strong association with that deceased person.

It is the practice to keep a vigil light burning at all times for the deceased, but it is not necessary. You may extinguish the candle after your prayer time is over and relight it the next day. The glass of water is changed every seven or nine days. As the water slowly evaporates during this period of time, it symbolizes your ancestors' drinking. It is not necessary to have pictures of your ancestors to have a formal shrine dedicated to them. All that is really needed is the water, candles, and your prayers. Many people use white flowers as an offering on their ancestral altar. Other offerings might include: fruit, a portion of cooked food (especially a favorite food of the ancestor), coffee, rum, wine, cigarettes, honey, cane syrup, pastries, or anything else that you feel they might like.

When cooking food specifically for the ancestors, meat should not be prepared. It is best to stay with cooked foods: potatoes, yams (sweet potatoes), white rice (not brown), other vegetables, fresh fruits, and breads are all good to give as offerings to the ancestors. However, do not add any salt to the food cooked for them. For some reason, the ancestors are not able to draw toward themselves any energy from the food cooked with salt, as food dries that has had salt added to it or that is cooked with it. Adding salt to the food is worse than not giving them food at all, since they are not able to draw energy from the food; they actually lose energy because of the presence of salt. Giving food to the ancestors, feeding them, is a way of strengthening them. As the ancestors grow in strength, they will speak to us more frequently. Other cultures have similar customs. It is a European practice to give a *dumb supper* at Halloween, in honor of the dead.

It will take at least six months of prayer and weekly offerings to begin to make any real contact in communicating with the ancestors. If you think that you hear "spirits" talking to you, avoid talking to them. Continue the offerings and ask for help and guidance, and thank them for the guidance they give. The reason you avoid speaking to any spirits who may be speaking to you is that while you may think it is your ancestors speaking, the voices you hear may be trickster spirits, and not your deceased relatives at all. In spite of your conviction that you can tell the difference between the voices of trickster spirits and your ancestors, you will not be able to do so.

The proof that you are communicating with your defunct blood relatives and not trickster spirits is that after about a year your life will be flowing in a smoother manner, with less trauma.

After you have done your daily prayers for the first nine days, you can begin to discuss your problems with your ancestors. Do not insult them by asking for help in buying a new outfit or a pair of shoes, or even to compel your lover to call you that night. It is appropriate to ask them to intervene only in life's serious problems, such as with the loss of a job, illness, etc. If you are not involved in a serious situation for the moment, simply ask them for continued guidance, health, prosperity for your home, and peace.

Honoring your ancestors is one-third of the power of a diviner priest or priestess. The other two-thirds of the power comes from your relationship with the nature and elemental spirits and from your relationship with Divinity.

CHAPTER 4

WORKING THE CANDLES

I n the previous chapter, "Honoring the Ancestors," an example was given of the types of offerings that were presented to deceased blood relatives. This offering is only given when it is revealed by sortilege/ divination that the ancestors want this offering in exchange for help with a problem. A live rooster is sacrificed to them in a ritual manner by a diviner priest/ess. The diviner priest/ess cannot set a fee for this service, as santeros may do in Santeria practice, but he or she may accept a donation if the family wishes to give one.

The saints, on the other hand, accept only fresh fruit, pastries, a glass of water, rum, gin, red or white wine, cooked foods such as red beans and rice, and cooked okra on rice. The head, legs and feet, heart, liver, gizzard, wing tips, and breast tip of a sacrificed rooster are cooked down in water until all the water is evaporated and everything starts to brown but not burn. The St. Joseph altars are a fine example of offerings to a saint.

CANDLES IN HISTORY

Before the invention of candles, small oil lamps called votive lamps were used in ancient temples and home shrines as the faithful addressed their prayers to the deities of old. When candles were first made they quickly replaced oil lamps in worship.

Candles made of beeswax were in use in Egypt and Crete as early as 3000 B.C.E. Relief carvings in ancient Egyptian tombs at Thebes show cone-shaped candles on dish-like holders, or candlesticks. The oldest-known archaeological finding of a candle fragment in Europe was near Avignon, France, dating from the first century C.E.

By the thirteenth century, guilds of chandlers or candle-makers were established. These craftsmen went from house to house in London and Paris, making candles. Beeswax or tallow (the processed suet, or hard fat, from cattle and sheep) was used for candles until around 1825. Natural dyes, used to color fabrics and other materials for more than 5,000 years, were blended into the beeswax or tallow as it melted, producing colored candles. Paraffin wax, the residue of crude oil distillation, was introduced in the 1850s, and is still widely used in making candles. Other nineteenth-century experiments produced candles from materials such as stearic acid, spermaceti, microcrystalline wax, and ceresin from petroleum.

The candles recommended here are preferred for religious ceremonies by Catholics of Latin and French descent. Seven-day candles were introduced around the turn of the twentieth century, replacing the common tapers previously used.

The practice of using a flame of some kind to accompany prayer is universal, a practice accepted and used in every major religion of the world except for Protestant Christianity. The few Protestants who do use candles with their prayers never admit this to their pastors or other church members. The pastor of a Protestant church would cry out loud, "This is against God." I believe they are wrong. Setting out lights as an offering with your prayer is not voodoo, it is not witchcraft, it is not satanism, as some would be tricked into believing out of ignorance and fear. It is simply an act of devotion. This devotional path is just one of the many paths that lead to God.

CANDLES AND PRAYER

The candles themselves act as an aid to help you focus your mind on your desires. All religions of a positive nature should encourage a person to bring their desires to God. The candles, when properly prepared, also represent your prayer. Therefore when using candles with your prayers, three elements come into focus:

- The candles are a physical representation of your prayer.

- Your mental concentration becomes more focused on your desire.

- Your emotions are backing up your words.

Someone once said to me that it is through the emotions that God is quickly reached. If your emotions cannot back up your words, they become dry and lifeless. Once the candles have been charged by your words and emotions, they continue to send forth the energy of your prayer and emotions as long as they are burning. This works on the same principle as if you take a brick, place it under a faucet, and let the faucet continuously drip, drip, drip on the brick. In time, the steady dripping of the water will make a hole in the brick. Constant pressure will bring positive results. Constant pressure will knock down the obstacles to your desires, opening the way for your prayer to be answered.

Some people, through lack of patience, tend to jinx their own prayers. They want results right away, and if they do not see things happening immediately, they think, this is not working, my prayers are not being heard, I'm wasting my time with this. In most cases this type of person wants something for nothing. Not all prayers are answered immediately. You will not always see results right away. In fact, in some instances it may seem that everything is going in just the opposite direction of what you are praying for. This is especially true if you are praying to break up a love affair, if your spouse is cheating on you and you want to save your marriage. Sometimes it is necessary for the two lovers to come closer together first, before they can have a big fallout sending them on their separate ways. Jinx your prayers with negative thinking and you will not get results. Maintain a positive attitude and mind, being patient in spite of the obstacles, and you will wake up one morning with your prayers answered. Thoughts are things, and all energy follows thought. The energy set in motion as the candles burn blends itself with the pattern of your thought or prayer. This is why it is important to remain in a positive frame of mind, knowing that your prayers will be answered with an attitude of expectation—expectation in the same sense as when you have ordered an item from a mail-order catalog and you are waiting for the UPS driver to deliver the package to your door.

Candles used in prayer vigils come in all shapes, sizes, and colors. Much has been written in the past about using stick candles. The candles recommended here are called seven-day vigil, novena candles, or seven-day candles. Fourteen-day candles are also available.

All the literature about candles mentions that the candles should be dressed with oil before they are lit. The seven-day vigil lights come encased in glass and are not dressed in the same fashion as one would dress a stick candle. A common method is to take a screwdriver and make a hole in the wax down along the side of the glass. Then fill the hole with oil and rub some of the oil around the top of the candle wax as you concentrate on your desire. If you are using the candle to bring something to yourself, then rub the oil in a clockwise direction. To banish or drive something away from you, rub the oil in a counterclockwise direction. Working with the seven-day lights is quite easy since you do not need to have candleholders. When the candles burn out, you simply put the empty glass in the garbage. There are no wax drippings to clean up.

THE SEVEN-DAY VIGIL LIGHTS

First among the seven-day vigil candles are those dedicated to a particular saint. The picture or a stencil of a saint will appear on one side of the jar and a prayer in English and Spanish will be printed on the other side. We commonly call these saint candles. You will not find a saint candle for all the saints listed in this book. When a candle is not available, the common practice is to use the color candle listed for the saint, placing a picture or prayer card next to the candle in its plain glass. All information pertaining to the saints listed in this book is from All Saints Chapel of Faith Spiritist Church.

The following saint candles can be purchased rather easily: Infant Jesus of Atocha (gold), Sacred Heart of Jesus (red or white), Our Lady of Charity (yellow), Hail Mary (blue or white), Our Lady of Guadelupe (pink or white), Our Lady of the Miraculous Medal (blue or white), Our Lady of Mount Carmel (white), Our Lady of Perpetual Help (white or blue), Our Lady of Regula (blue), St. Anne (white), St. Barbara (red), St. Clare of Assisi (white), St. Dymphna (blue), St. Lucy (white or blue), St. Martha (green or white), St. Rita (white), St. Therese (yellow), San Alejo/St. Alex (pink), St. Anthony of Padua (brown, green, or orange, St. Expidite (yellow), St. Francis of Assisi (brown), St. Cipriano (purple), St. Ignatius of Loyola (white), St. John the Baptist (brown or green), St. Joseph (white or yellow), St. Jude (white, red, or green), St. Martin Caballero (red), St. Martin de Porres (purple or white), St. Peter (white or red), St. Lazarus (yellow), Guardian Angel (white), St. Michael the Archangel (red, purple, or green).

Adam and Eve

This candle comes in red and pink. The pink is used to help initiate a romance or a friendship. Burning this candle can help you to be liked by all people. The red candle is used to bring two people or a married couple closer together.

Ajo Macho

This is a green candle. It is used to restore health, bring good fortune, and turn evil away.

Allan Kardec

This candle is two-colored: gold and green. It is burned for spiritual guidance, to protect your luck, to keep evil and harm away.

Anima Sola/Lonely Soul

This is a red-colored candle. It is burned to bring back lost things, for lost or unrequited love. This candle should be burned when you have a spirit in the house. It is said to bring peace to people who are mentally disturbed.

Attraction

Another red candle. This is an all-purpose candle used for attracting love, money, and health, or to keep a person attracted to you.

Bayberry

This is a seven-day, bayberry-scented green candle. It is used as a money-drawing candle and to help keep prosperity in the home.

Better Business

Another two-colored candle, gold and green. It is used to help keep business activity flowing.

Black Cat

You can find this candle in black or white. It is used to change one's bad luck to good.

Black Tobacco

This is a voodoo candle in which a mixture of herbs is added along with black tobacco. It is used to win stubborn court cases and to keep you on another's mind.

Block Buster

This type of candle combines two colors: dark red and black, gold and pink, or pink and green. The Block Buster is best when used with a reversible candle. The colors used depend on the situation. All of the Block Buster candles are used to break up any work that someone has put on you to jinx your life.

Break Up

This candle comes in white, black, or red. The black candle is the most popular in our store. It is used to break up any friendship or love affair. The white Break Up candle can be used with the black color as a substitute for a gray-colored candle. The red Break Up candle, when prepared to give out a negative vibration, is used to create strife, arguments, and war between two people.

Buda

The Buda candle is found in either pink, gold, or green. The pink Buda candle is used for marriage. The green Buda is for family, harmony, health, peace, and posterity. The gold Buda is burned for wealth and strength. One woman told me that she uses the pink Buda to bring straying husbands back to their wives.

Chameleon

This is a red candle. It is burned for good fortune, luck in love.

Chango Macho

This gold-colored candle is used to change bad luck to good fortune.

Chuparosa

One style is red, the other type is two-colored, red and green. The red Chuparosa is for lost love, while the red and green is for good luck.

Come to Me

This candle comes in red. It is used to bring a person to you. Some people burn this candle with a Money Drawing or Fast Luck candle if this is what the person wants to come to them.

Commanding

This is a purple candle used to control another, to gain power over another.

Controlling

Comes only in orange. It is used to help keep children under control or when you want to get someone to do what you want. Use with a yellow and green Money and a green and black Reversible to get a raise in pay.

Cross of Caravaca

This yellow candle is known as the Wishing Cross. When used with a tonka bean, it brings good luck, and opens your roads.

Court Case

Comes in either blue or brown. This candle is used to win a court case. The brown Court Case candle can be used to confuse any testimony against you.

Divine Savior

This is a red candle burned for general protection.

Don Pedrito

This candle comes in white and is used in times of sickness.

DUME

This candle comes only in black. Use to get revenge on another. Cause bad luck by blocking another's path.

Fast Luck

You will find this candle in green, and in two colors, gold and green, or pink and green. It is burned to bring luck in a hurry. Use in combination with other candles. It also comes in seven colors.

Ellegua

White is the color of this candle. It is used to delay a court case or lawsuit, and to protect you from a lawsuit against you.

Get Away

A two-colored candle in black and red. Burn to put away someone who is bothering you, to cause another to move out of the home, get out of your life, to cause a troublesome neighbor to move, or to stop an ex-lover's harassment.

Helping Hand

This candle comes in seven different colors or a solid green. It is used to receive general blessings for love, money, health, etc.

High John the Conqueror

You will find this candle in either a solid purple or in three colors: purple, orange, and purple. It is used to conquer another, bring good fortune, or draw money.

Holy Trinity

This candle is yellow. It is burned for special requests, to escape jail, for protection from evil.

Indian Spirit

This candle is red. It is used as an offering to Indian spirits for courage, protection, and to turn away evil magick.

Job

A two-colored candle, pink and green. Burn when looking for work or to succeed and prosper in your present job.

Hunchback

A red candle burned to bring good fortune or to have gambling luck.

Just Judge

This candle comes in either white or red. The white candle is used to influence the judge's decision in your favor, and also for protection from your enemies. The red Just Judge is used to get a divorce.

King Solomon

You will find this candle in a purple color. Burn for domination and control, giving you power over others.

Law Stay Away

This two-color candle is gray and brown. Used by those involved in illegal businesses, to stop harassment by the police. To break up a jinxed condition—when you are always being stopped by the police or in danger of losing your driver's license or going broke by paying for too many traffic tickets.

Lodestone

This multipurpose candle only comes in red. It is burned to draw to you love, money, health, when used in combination with other candles. The other candle will represent the desire or object you desire drawn to you.

Lucky Bingo

You will find this candle in green or a gold and green combination. It is best used in a combination such as a green Lucky

Bingo with a Lodestone candle and a gold and green Money-Drawing candle. Or a combination of a gold-green Lucky Bingo, with an orange Controlling, and a pink and green Money Drawing.

Money Drawing

This candle comes in several types, in a seven-color candle, in solid green, in gold and green, and pink and green. Used when you need to draw money.

Nino Fidencio

This is a white candle. People who invoke this saint do so for general protection or for special requests.

One Drop of Luck

This two-colored candle in gold and green is used for all games of chance.

Pancho Villa

This is a red candle, used to draw customers to a business. Add a Protection candle with it to protect a business from being jinxed.

Peaceful Home

You will find this candle in two colors, blue and white. It is used to settle disturbing conditions in the home. Some users add a Reversible candle with it, along with a Protection candle, when there are a lot of arguments and fighting in the home.

Protection Candle

Comes in black, white, red, and purple. Also known as Protection from Enemies. Used to give protective energy from the evil and harm that your enemies want to see happen to you, from jealousy and the evil eye.

Reversible

This candle is available in three combinations: white and black, red and black, and green and black. It is used to reverse and send back the evil and harm to the person who is causing your bad luck. The green and black combination is used to reverse financial difficulty; the white and black to reverse any misfortune from envy and the evil eye; the red and black when someone is interfering with your love life.

Run Devil Run

This candle may be either white, black, or red. Burn it if you are having a string of bad luck, when things are always going wrong and you have a dark cloud hanging over your head.

Sacred Heart of Jesus

This candle is available in red or white. It is used for daily blessings.

Seven African Powers

You will find this candle in seven different colors. Burn it as a multipurpose candle for general blessings in all areas of your life.

Steady Work

This candle comes in green and orange. Use it to keep your job, if you are self-employed, or in cases of a layoff due to business slowing down.

Success

This is a pink candle. It is burned with another to symbolize the desire of your life that you want success in.

Three Skulls

You will see this candle in either white, black, or red. White is used for peace and tranquility. Red is used for love or to bring back a strayed lover. Black is used for doing evil or to change your luck.

Uncrossing

This candle comes in either purple or white. Burn it to remove negative or crossed conditions.

Other candles manufactured by Nite Glow Candle Company that are not included in the above list are:

Black Cat

Nite Glow's black candle comes in white, black, or seven colors. It is used to change bad luck to good.

Bleeding Heart

A white candle used to begin a love affair.

Casino/Gamblers

This is a green candle burned to have luck in the casinos.

Do As I Say

This is a two-colored candle in orange and purple. It is used to command and control another. To get others to listen to you and cooperate.

Easy Street

This is a green candle used in combination with other candles to keep money flowing to you.

Go Away Evil

This candle comes in two colors: black and purple. It is burned to hold back the evil another wants to send to you. Used with an Uncrossing to break up an evil condition.

Health

This white candle is burned with an Ajo Macho to help regain or maintain health.

House Blessing

This is a blue candle used to help you hold on to your money, to keep money in the home. It is burned with a Money Drawing candle.

Intranquil Spirit

This red candle is burned to draw to yourself a wandering love, or to keep you on another's mind. It is best when burned with a Black Tobacco candle.

Jinx Removing

You will find this candle in black or in three colors: gray, pink, and green. Use it to break up a jinxed condition, or prevent another from jinxing your money and love.

Juan Minero

This is a red candle. It is burned for health purposes and special requests.

Love Drawing

A two-colored candle in pink and red. It is used to strengthen a love affair. To keep your mate at home.

Lucky Lottery

This candle comes in green. It is burned for luck in playing the lottery.

Make Your Wish

This is a pink candle used for special requests to be answered.

Money Release

This green-colored candle is used in combination with other candles when someone owes you money and doesn't want to pay you back. To get a raise in pay on the job.

Pay Me

Another green candle used to get back money that is owed.

Peace

This white candle is burned for peace of mind when used with a St. Dymphna, or with a Reversible in red and black if you want peace in your life.

Road Opener

You will find this candle in three colors: orange, green, and gold. It is best used with a Purple Uncrossing and a Reversible to remove blocks preventing your luck and money flowing to you. Start new projects.

Secret Desires

Comes in two colors: pink and blue. It is burned for special requests.

Shut Your Mouth

This blue and black candle is burned with a St. Ramon candle for stopping gossip.

Twenty-third Psalm

A white candle used for special requests.

PLAIN GLASS SEVEN-DAY VIGILS

These candles have proven to be practical when used in candle burning rituals, in place of the household or stick candles. When the ritual is finished there are no wax drippings or candle holders to clean up. Simply throw the glass jars in the garbage. You will find them in twelve basic colors. Burn them for the problems or purposes indicated.

Black

Sadness and mourning, evil, loss, discord, confusion.

Brown

Hesitation in all matters, uncertainty and doubt, neutrality, robs energy.

Blue

Understanding, health, tranquility, protection, peace, general happiness, patience, spiritual awareness, compassion.

Gray

Cancellation, stalemate, neutrality. It is traditional to use a white and black together if gray is not available.

Green

Money, luck, financial success and prosperity, fertility, good crops and harvest, cooperation, healing.

Orange

Encouragement, strengthen ability to concentrate, attraction, adaptability, stimulation, positive changes.

Pink

Overcomes evil, represents honor, love, morality, friendship, general success and harmony, joy.

Purple

Ambition, promotes business progress, power, causes tension, expands what you already have, spirituality.

Red

Love, sexuality, health, strength physical vigor, lust and passion, energy, attraction, and drawing.

White

Breaks curses and crossed conditions, represents faith, purity, truth, and sincerity.

Yellow and Gold

Attraction, persuasion, confidence, charm, joy, uplifting thoughts.

Seven Colors

Available in plain glass for general blessings in luck, love, health, money, etc.

Three-Color Plain Glass

Comes in red, white, and blue. We call this a victory candle.

CANDLES OF A NEGATIVE INFLUENCE

These candles are made by the person intending to use them. They simply represent the negative quality of a positive color, easily made by applying black wax on the top of a plain seven-day candle. This type of candle is useful in rituals to banish a negative condition such as jealousy or infidelity in a relationship. The opposite is also true in bringing a negative or hexing condition to a situation. The candles are as follows:

Blue

Lack of emotions, depression, frigidity, apathy, sorrow and gloom, tears and weeping, melancholy, loss of love.

Green

Jealousy, envy, avarice and greed, disharmony, suspicion, resentment.

Orange

Inconsistency, adultery, perfidy, cowardice, distrust.

Yellow

Illness and disease, decay, sickly appearance, adultery, cowardice, lack of ambition.

Red

Hatred, anger, anarchy, war, violence, cruelty and revenge, arguments.

White

Corruption and debility, lack of strength and vigor, infirmity, weakness, timidity, impotence, impurity, lack of life, lack of ambition.

A negative condition is anything that is of detriment, injury, damage, sabotage and ruin, abuse, slander and libel, discouragement, derogatory and defamatory influence, or maligning.

Thoughts of despair, depression, pessimism, melancholy, despondency, sadness, discouragement are all negative.

People are negative who oppose and obstruct, limit, impede, block and hinder, are spiteful, bear rancour, are hateful, or hold grudges. Animosity and malice are negative in character.

It is commonly believed that thoughts are things. A person's constant, dominant thoughts enter the heart through the subconscious mind. It is the thoughts in the heart that God sees, thus giving truth to the saying: "As a man thinketh, so he is in his heart." The thoughts imbedded within the subconscious mind are constantly reinforced by the constant thoughts of the conscious mind. Consequently, if the thoughts within the conscious mind are always negative in nature, any thought contrary to the negative belief will be automatically blocked from manifesting itself. The subconscious only sends out to Divinity/Deity the beliefs it holds, creating your life's pattern or present condition, whether positive or negative, with no respect of persons. Therefore, negative thoughts produce negative life experiences. Positive thoughts produce positive life experiences. Through our own minds we bless or curse our own lives. This negative condition is a form of self-sabotage and ruin. It is important to learn how to transform negative thought patterns into positive ones. The subconscious always believes as fact the reinforcing thought of the conscious. The subconscious must be tricked into believing that the negative thought is changed into the positive. If you can change your thoughts you can change your life. On pages 89 and 90 you will find directions for conducting a ritual of transformation and a diagram showing the candle layout for this ritual.

RITUAL OF TRANSFORMATION

1. A zodiac or astral candle representing the person.

2. A seven-color plain glass vigil candle representing the person's chakras. Between these two candles you will place a poppet or other object belonging to the individual.

3. A yellow and pink Block Buster, symbolizing attracting morality, love, and friendship into the person's life.

4. A pink and blue Secret Desire candle to symbolize the person overcoming evil as she or he gains understanding and spiritual awareness.

5. A white candle representing the virtue of truth and sincerity, and pure faith coming into the person's life. For this candle you use the 23rd Psalm. On it is written the Ten Commandments, the Lord's Prayer, and the Twenty-third Psalm.

6. A purple candle or a King Solomon, representing spiritual power.

7. An orange or a Controlling candle for positive change, objectivity, courage, conquering fear.

8. A blue candle representing the quality of patience and compassion.

9. A negative green, and a negative red, both red and green symbolizing the negative traits and emotions you desire to transform into a positive trait.

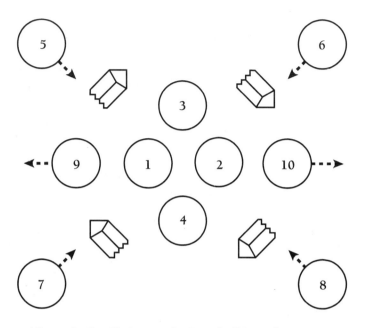

Figure 1. Candle Layout for Ritual of Transformation

This ritual is best begun on the night of the full moon, as you move candles 9 and 10 one or two inches away from candles 1 and 2. Once candles 9 and 10 are burned out, they are not replaced. Candles 1 through 4, and 5 through 8, are replaced by new candles as needed. These candles are left to burn for the duration of the waning phases of the moon. This completes part one of the Ritual of Transformation. Part two begins on the night of the new moon. The negative red and green candles are completely left out of the pattern. Each day, candles 5 through 8 are moved one to two inches toward candles 1 and 2, which are always left stationary.

This ritual is supplemented every three days with a spiritual bath and smoking or fumigation of the body.

Warning!

You cannot change a person's character; no human being has this power. Only an individual has the ability to change their own negative qualities by persistent prayer, meditation, and spiritual cleansing. Change does not come overnight and in most cases may even take a year of daily practice. This can be painful for some people because changing negative thoughts and emotions may seem to them as though a part of their self is dying, to be reborn as a new creature. Wanting to change another's character is the beginning of problems in a relationship. Too many times, a woman sees a man, and she sees only the potential of what he could be. The woman falls in love, not with the man, but with the potential. As she tries to change the man to fit the potential, naturally the man will rebel, and problems will begin to take root. It is far better to love and accept a person as he or she actually is than to try to change them. It is far better to have the courage to let go of a relationship when the other does not have the qualities that you are looking for than to try to change the person.

And so I leave you with a few words from Galatians, chapter 5, about negative and positive actions and emotions:

> Verses 19–21: "Now the works of the flesh are obvious: immorality, impurity, licentiousness, idolatry, sorcery (acts of negative magic against another), hatreds, rivalry, jealousy, outbursts of fury, occasions of envy, drinking bouts, orgies, and the like."

Verses 22–23: "In contrast, the fruit of the Spirit is love, joy, peace, patience, kindness, generosity, faithfulness, gentleness, self-control. Against such there is no law."

Therefore, anyone able to adopt the positive attitude and emotions mentioned in verses 22 and 23 does have the Holy Spirit within them, regardless of their religious belief, or whether they accept Jesus or not. I have personally known Hindi, Bhuddists, and Witches, all of whom have proven to be a better class of people than those I have known who profess, "love thy neighbor" and are filled with hate, prejudice, and anger.

CHAPTER 5

THE LANGUAGE OF CANDLES

hen praying with your candle it is good to observe its flame, the presence of wafts of smoke, and the color, if the glass is turning black inside, if the glass breaks, etc. Each of these signs has its own meaning. This is the spirit telling you something about your work or of a present condition in your life, if your prayer will be granted, or if spiritual blockages are not yet completely removed so that your prayer will be answered.

HOW THE CANDLE BURNS

When you first light the candle, if it emits black smoke it is a sign that it is beginning to remove negative energy from your desire. When the smoke is white, then your prayer will be answered, but there may be some struggles to obtain your desire.

A strong flame is a good indication. The candle is working by sending out a lot of power and energy to bring about a manifestation of your prayer. This is a sign that the candle is working rapidly.

A weak or low flame indicates that the candle is working very slowly to remove an obstacle or to bring in a positive vibration to your prayer. You are facing some heavy opposition to having the request granted. It is an indication that you will have to pray a little longer time before your desire is granted.

A jumping flame can indicate spiritual warfare on your behalf. A lot of raw energy and power is working. If the candle is a war candle, then the person whose name is attached to the candle is fighting.

If the smoke wafts toward you, then your prayer is acknowledged.

If the smoke blows in the direction away from you, it is a definite sign that you still need perseverance in order to obtain your desire.

If the smoke turns toward your right, then you will need to use a bit of patience, success will come through using your head.

Again if the smoke turns toward you, success will come quickly in granting the prayer.

If the smoke blows toward your left, then you are becoming too emotionally involved with the situation you are praying for and in danger of subconsciously sabotaging your own prayer so that it will not be answered.

At times you will hear crackling sounds as the candles are burning. This is taken to indicate that the spirit is pleading your case on your behalf. The stronger the crackling sound, the stronger the opposition is against you.

If the glass breaks, it can indicate, depending on the situation, that someone is working against you because the pressure is on. On the other hand, if the work you are doing is an uncrossing or jinx removing and the glass breaks, then the evil that is against you is broken.

Reading the Glass

If the glass containing the candle remains clear as it burns (Figure 2), your prayer will be granted in spite of any opposition.

If the glass begins to turn black at the top but is clearing up on the bottom (Figure 3), it is a sign that you have someone working against you. The darker it turns, the stronger the opposition. This does not mean your prayer will not be answered. Don't jinx yourself with negative thinking here; your prayer can still be answered with perseverance.

Figure 2.

Figure 3.

If the glass turns black all the way down to the bottom (Figure 4), you have some serious obstacles blocking your prayer from coming into reality. You need to do some uncrossing lights on yourself, and take some spiritual baths to remove negativity and the jinxed condition. You are a victim of black magick. If you are unlucky, consult a diviner priest or priestess; if you belong to the Santeria religion, consult either a Babalawo or the Santero who is your godfather in the religion. You may need a stronger counter-work than just using candles and spiritual baths to remove this type of strong negative work.

Figure 4.

IN WORKING THE CANDLES

In other books written on candle burning, authors have used as their examples household or stick candles. These books also contain patterns for arranging the candles. In each pattern certain candles are moved toward or away from the candle representing the petitioner. This commonly taught method is a contemporary form of sympathetic magick, in which like attracts like. It is often the easiest form of sympathetic magick because it is not always necessary to have a personal object such as hair or clothing belonging to the people represented in the pattern. Usually all that is used is a zodiac or astral candle of the person with their name and birthdate written in the candle wax. With this technique you can do effective magick without arousing suspicion in trying to get a personal object from another. You can do your work in complete secrecy, not letting the left hand know what the right hand is doing. If you are lucky enough to obtain some personal items or even a picture of the person, attaching the items to the zodiac or astral candle will cause it to succumb more easily to the influence given off by the other candles.

Seven-day vigil lights are not usually set in a pattern in which the candles are moved either away or toward the petitioners. The vigil lights are set up in a line on your altar, along with a saint candle, before a statue or picture of the saint you intend to invoke for assistance. Traditionally the candles are left burning continuously until they burn themselves out. They are usually not extinguished. As the candles burn, the glass becomes hot to the touch.

As a safety precaution some people place the candles in a large aluminum baking pan or cookie sheet filled with a layer of sand on the bottom. If the candle glass breaks, the wax will drip in the pan, mixing and hardening with the sand. However, the candle glass does not break often because the glass itself is quite thick.

Most often, when working with the seven-day vigils, a zodiac or astral candle is not used. The name(s) of the person(s) involved is written on paper and the paper placed under the candle itself or taped to its side. Some people will try to use only one seven-day vigil candle to obtain their desire, but it is best to use the candles in combinations representing the entire situation. For example, a young lady wishes to obtain the love of a certain gentleman, but unfortunately the man is involved with another. The young lady then decides to put a Break Up light on the couple. To do so, she will write on a piece of paper the names of the couple either three, five, seven, or nine times, and place the paper under the Break Up light. The consistent pressure from the light and the young lady's prayer for the couple to break up may be answered by the couple breaking up. However, there is no guarantee that the gentleman will come to the young lady because she did not put up a light to draw him toward her. Therefore, if the gentleman broke off his relationship with the first woman but is currently seeing another instead of the young lady who wanted him, by working with only one candle, she obtained only half of her desire. It is best to represent the entire situation by the vigil lights.

Most people will consult a diviner priest/ess to see exactly which type of candles are to be used, or if any existing pattern needs to be modified in some way to fit their particular problem.

In this type of candle burning, altar candles and zodiac or astral candles are not used. Individual names pertaining to the situation are written on paper three, five, seven, or nine times. After each name one word indicating the desire is also written. For example: Jane Doe/love. It is common practice to write the names of two people on one piece of paper. In this case one person's name is written on top of the other's name. For example: Jane Doe has been dating John Smith for three years. She feels that it is time for them to get married. The paper containing the essence of her prayer (to be placed under her candle) would look like this when written properly:

Jane Smith/marriage

Jane Smith/marriage

Jane Smith/marriage

This may look like indecipherable scribble, but Jane Doe's name is actually written on top of John Smith's name and the word "marriage" follows each name. As Jane Doe writes each name, it is important that she pray for her desire to be granted.

Let us say that, after three years of marriage, John Smith began seeing another woman. Jane Doe found out about the other woman, but she still wants to hold on to her marriage, so she decides to break up this new romance. The names of her husband and the other woman would be placed under a break up light. Jane Doe would write the names crossing each other or going in opposite directions. The paper would look like this:

John Smith/separate
John Smith/separate
John Smith/separate

Alice Homewrecker/separate
Alice Homewrecker/separate
Alice Homewrecker/separate

The writing would look like this when crossing each other:

John Smith/separate
John Smith/separate
John Smith/separate

Alice Homewrecker/separate
Alice Homewrecker/separate
Alice Homewrecker/separate

Usually the person whose name is written on top of the other person's will have a dominant role in bringing about the desire. In the case of working to separate two people it does not matter whose name is on top.

WARNING: When doing ritual work to obtain the love of a specific person, there is a trap. You will take the risk of being more in love with the other person than that person is in love with you. In this case you may not have peace of mind in the relationship because negative emotions such as jealousy and distrust will surface, sabotaging the relationship.

In writing the names of people, it is traditional to use an odd number, but it does not matter which odd number is used. To say that names have to be written seven times only is bordering on superstition.

When it comes to prayers, it is also traditional to say an odd number of prayers. The saying goes: "To say a prayer three times, it will be answered once. To say a prayer seven times, those who hear it will begin to believe it. To say a prayer nine times, it will be answered." In reality, anything worth praying for is done persistently over a period of time, until the request is granted. The candles, combined with prayer, set up a pressure to bring about the needed change in order for the prayer to be answered. It is the consistent pressure that will knock down the obstacles. This does require patience and faith that, in spite of the obstacles in your way, the prayer will be answered in your favor. You will not often see any change immediately. If you do not see change happening immediately in the way you have in mind it should, you may risk sabotaging your prayer. To think that what you are doing is not working is setting up a silent prayer for failure. Patience, a positive attitude, and perseverance are needed to bring positive results.

PROBLEM-SOLVING CANDLE RITUALS

In the following pages are suggested candle combinations and rituals for addressing fifty-seven different types of problems that people may encounter in life. These are only basic combinations and may need to be modified by adding or subtracting a candle to fit the person's particular situation. When you are instructed to write your name or another's, or other words, the paper on which the words are written should be placed under the candle or taped to its side.

To Stop Gossip
Gossip is powerful enough to create a lot of problems for an individual. This is a case where the person is being hexed

by the tongue. When a lie is said consistently about another, other people will begin to believe the lie. To stop gossip, you will need:

1. Pink Adam and Eve candle, dressed with Dragon Blood oil. Write your name on paper and place the paper under the candle or tape it to the side of the candle. If you do not know the name of the person who is gossiping about you, write: "All detrimental talk about me is now stopped."

2. Shut Your Mouth candle, dressed with Jinx Removing oil. Sprinkle a bit of slippery elm in the candle. Write the name of the person who is gossiping.

3. Uncrossing candle, dressed with Uncrossing oil. Sprinkle a bit of five-finger grass (cinquefoil) on the candle. Write your name for this candle.

4. With your prayer from the heart you should also pray Psalm 47, to be liked by all people, and Psalms 2 and 31, for the gossip to be stopped.

5. A suggested spiritual bath to take would be made from slippery elm bark and five-finger grass.

To Hold On to Your Money

Many times your money will flow out of your hands as fast as it comes in. Perhaps someone is jinxing your money.

1. House Blessing candle dressed with Money oil. Write your name for this candle.

2. Money Drawing candle dressed with Money oil. Again write your name.

3. Green and Black Reversible candle, dressed with Dragon Blood oil. In the green wax, you will write your name. On paper write: "Financial difficulties are put away from me."

4. Burn garlic peels on the stove in your kitchen to keep money in the home. Some people make a small charm by wrapping a dollar bill around a piece of John the Conqueror root and a two-inch piece of vencedor wood (what we call the Lilac Chaste tree is vencedor). A small anchor charm is tied to this bundle with orange string, and the bundle placed between the House Blessing and the Money Drawing candles as they burn.

5. Psalms 4 and 41 are suggested; read them three times each. If you keep telling yourself that you never have money, you will always be broke. A spiritual bath may be taken using Money-Drawing herbs and 1 cup of Epsom salt, ½ cup of table salt, ¼ cup of baking soda, 1 cup of apple cider vinegar, ¼ cup of green bath and floor wash.

To Get Someone Out of Jail

This is also useful if the person is already in jail and is going before the parole board to discuss their release.

1. St. Jude candles, one white, one red, one green, dressed with St. Jude oil. Write the name of the person who is in jail.

2. Holy Trinity candle dressed with Holy oil. Again write the person's name.

3. 23rd Psalm candle, dressed with Holy oil. Write the name of the person who is in jail.

4. Controlling candle, dressed with Controlling oil. Write the person's name.

5. Success candle, dressed with Success oil. Write the person's name. A picture of the individual who is in jail is placed in a small jar. Added to this is are 3 tablespoons of white sugar, 1 teaspoon of galangal, cascara sagrada, ¼ stick of cinnamon. Cover the jar. Each day as you pray for the person's release, you shake the jar.

6. For a decision to be made in favor of the one in jail, Psalm 71 is suggested, repeated seven times, followed by Psalm 20.

To Protect an Incarcerated Person from Harm or Danger

With the overcrowding of jails, tempers can flare up easily. Fights will break out and someone may be hurt or even killed. Sometimes a person on the outside will even pay another inmate to kill a particular inmate while both are incarcerated.

1. St. Barbara candle, dressed with Holy oil or St. Barbara oil. Write the incarcerated person's name on paper.

2. Protection candle, dressed with Protection oil. Write the person's name.

3. Reversible (red and black), dressed with Dragon Blood oil. Write the person's name in the red wax, on paper write "secret plots to harm (name) are stopped."

4. Guardian Angel candle, dressed with Holy oil. Write the person's name.

5. Adam and Eve (pink) candle, dressed with Peace oil. Write the person's name.

6. Suggested Psalms are number 7, to protect someone from the secret plots of others that would harm them, Psalm 47 to be liked by all, Psalm 9 to protect from evil and danger, and finally, Psalm 130 for safety.

7. A picture of the incarcerated person is placed in a small box. Over the picture sprinkle: five-finger grass (cinquefoil), a teaspoon of brown sugar, and a teaspoon of hyssop.

To Win a Court Case

Lawyers and the courts are always busy. If you are not in court trying to get a divorce, someone may be suing you for some reason. This type of work can be a little complicated.

1. Court Case (blue for criminal cases) candle, dressed with Court oil. Write the name of the person who is going to court, and their attorney's name.

2. Success candle, dressed with Success oil. Write the person's name.

3. Just Judge (white) candle, dressed with Rose oil. Write the judge's name and the attorney's name.

4. If someone is suing you: Gold candle, dressed with Success oil. Write your name or the name of the person going to court.

5. If another is testifying against you: Brown candle, dressed with Confusion oil. Add a pinch of five-finger grass (cinquefoil) in the candle. Write the name of the person who is testifying and sprinkle some five-finger grass on the paper with their name, to confuse their testimony,

6. If you are going to divorce court: Just Judge (red) candle, dressed with Rose oil. Write the judge's name and your attorney's name.

7. Court Case (brown for civil offenses). Suggested Psalms: 35 and 36 to win your case. Psalm 7 if you have a strong and bitter opponent. Psalm 93 for help in court cases. Carry a piece of Chewing John in your pocket. Before entering the courtroom break off a small piece and chew it, spitting out the juice in the court room so that your words are believed.

To Protect From a Jinxed Condition

This is a set-up you should keep going at all times. You never know when someone is trying to work against you by throwing a monkey wrench in your plans.

1. Reversible candle, dressed with Dragon Blood oil. In the wax at the top, write your name. On paper you should write: "All evil and harm that is sent to me reverses back to my enemies 3 x 3." This paper goes on the bottom of the Reversible candle.

2. Uncrossing (purple) candle, dressed with Uncrossing oil. Write your name.

3. Guardian Angel candle, dressed with Holy oil. Write your name. Suggested Psalms are numbers 53, 54, and 55, followed by number 70. A good spiritual bath to take periodically is made with nutmeg, hydrangea, and hyssop.

To Hold On to Your Mate

When it comes to love, some people can be quite fickle. You may have to deal with a person who only wants to date married people. You may have to deal with someone deliberately trying to break up a relationship. Yes, even blood relatives will try to use magick to break up a relationship or prevent two people from getting married.

1. Love Drawing candle, dressed with Strong Love oil. Write both your name and your lover's name.

2. Reversible (red and black) candle, dressed with Dragon Blood oil. In the red wax write your initials and your lover's initials. Around the initials draw a heart. On paper write the name of the person trying to break up your romance. If you don't know the person's name, write: "All rivals to my relationship are removed."

3. Come to Me candle, dressed with Love oil or Come to Me oil. Write both your name and your lover's name.

4. Place a picture of your lover in a jar. Over the picture sprinkle spikenard herb, rose petals, and hyssop.

5. Suggested Psalms are 139 and 140 to keep your romance strong, and Psalm 113 to remove infidelity in a mate.

To Maintain Health

In our busy, hectic schedules it is not always easy to eat a balanced meal. Many people have a diet of fast food and vitamin pills. It is commonly believed that disease begins within the spiritual body of the person and remains attached to the aura before its symptoms begin to manifest in the physical body. Of course, this ritual will not protect your health from the physical harm due to a car accident, or from falling and breaking a bone, but this ritual does provide spiritual protection to keep you from getting colds and influenza, which is especially useful for those working in a health field. Many people who must always be around sick people, some with contagious diseases, never catch the illnesses themselves and can testify to the ritual's effectiveness.

1. Ajo Macho candle, dressed with Health oil. Write your name.

2. Health candle, dressed with Health oil. Write your name.

3. Victory candle, dressed with Health oil. Write your name.

4. In this setup the colors to be used are green for healing, blue for health, red for strength and physical vigor, and white for breaking up or protecting from the crossed condition of illness. Some people put a toe of garlic and a vitamin pill in each candle. They also take a garlic capsule and a vitamin daily to help create a greater link between themselves and the vibratory influence given off by the candles themselves.

5. A general type of spiritual bath that may be taken is made with eucalyptus, carnation flowers, and rue.

To Obtain Daily Blessings

We should all offer daily prayer for our lives to be blessed so that we may prosper in what we are doing. This is part of a daily devotion to the saints. For the seven African Powers, the orishas are invoked only by those in Santeria. The Catholic saint pictured is invoked instead, forming a litany to the saints combined with those pictured on the Helping Hand candle. The saints are: the Blessed Mother, St. Joseph, St. Ann, St. Joachim, the Infant Jesus (pictured on the Helping Hand candle), Our Lady of Mercy, Our Lady Of Regla, Our Lady of Charity, St. Barbara, St. Francis of Assisi, St. John the Baptist, and St. Anthony of Padua. Some people will also add to this setup a Guardian Angel and the Holy Trinity. This daily devotional is done for only seven days each month, always beginning the devotional on the first Fridays of each month, for example. The calendar date can be disregarded because the first Friday of each month would not be on the same day of each month.

1. Seven African Powers candle, dressed with Honeysuckle oil or Fast Luck oil. Write your name for this candle.

2. Sacred Heart of Jesus candle, dressed with Holy oil. Again write your name three, five, seven, or nine times.

3. Helping Hand candle, dressed with Helping Hand oil or Fast Luck oil. Write your name.

4. Suggested spiritual bath would be a Seven Holy Herb bath.

5. Recite Psalms 57 and 73 through 83.

To Overcome Addictions of Alcohol and Drugs

It is sad to be bound to someone with alcohol or drug problems. The addiction places a heavy burden upon the rest of the family members, adding unnecessary worry and stress.

Drug-related:

1. St. Lazarus candle, dressed with Jinx Removing oil. Write the addicted person's name.

2. Black Jinx Removing candle, dressed with Jinx Removing oil. Again write the person's name.

3. St. Jude candle, dressed with St. Jude oil. Write the person's name.

Alcohol related:

1. St. Clare candle, dressed with Uncrossing oil. Write the person's name.

2. Jinx Removing (black) candle, dressed with jinx removing oil. Again write the person's name.

3. St. Jude candle, dressed with St. Jude oil. Write the person's name. Place a personal item belonging to the
person in a jar. Take one tablespoon of each type of
alcohol the person drinks, mix this with equal parts of
Four Thieves Vinegar (recipe below), and ½ teaspoon of
Angelica root. Place all in the bottle, and each day shake
the bottle as you pray for the person to get so sick that
they will stop drinking altogether. Suggested Psalms:
25, 26, and 37.

Four Thieves Vinegar: To a gallon of strong cider vinegar, add
a handful of each of the following: rosemary, wormwood,
lavender, rue, sage, and mint. Add one ounce of powdered
camphor gum. Tightly close the container with the cider and
herbs in it. Place this container in a pan of water and heat until
the water begins to boil. Always shake this mixture before
heating. Heat the mixture daily for four days. Strain the herbs
from the liquid, bottle the liquid, and keep it tightly closed.
(Reprinted by permission from *Charms, Spells & Formulas* by
Ray T. Malbrough (Llewellyn Publications, 1986).)

To Strengthen Your Romance

Once a friendship is started, it may need a little boost to get it going in the right direction. Sometimes even when attraction is there, one of the intended is a bit shy.

1. Adam and Eve (red) candle, dressed with Strong Love oil. Write your name on top of the lover's name.

2. Road Opener candle, dressed with Road Opener oil or High John the Conqueror oil. Write both names for this candle. Or, substitute a Cross of Caravaca candle with one tonka bean dressed with Compelling oil.

3. Chuparosa (red and green) candle, dressed with Strong Love oil. Write both names again.

4. Call out the lover's full name three times, then say Psalm 138, and after each verse pray that the love will grow stronger as the moon grows to full. Finish with Psalm 16 three times, and Psalm 139.

5. Every Friday take a Love Drawing spiritual bath with rose petals, parsley flakes, and lavender, sweetened with 1 teaspoon of honey.

To Stop Infidelity

It's no fun when you are sitting at home and your mate is out "tomcatting around." The thought of possibly catching a sexually transmitted disease from a bedmate who is preoccupied with spreading his or her love around is terrifying. To have some peace of mind try this.

1. Adam and Eve (red) candle, dressed with Love and spikenard oils mixed. Write both your name and your mate's name on paper. Place it under the candle.

2. Gray colored candle, dressed with Break Up oil. Write your mate's name.

3. A Negative yellow (representing infidelity) candle, dressed with Double Cross oil. Write your mate's name.

4. Come to Me candle, dressed with Come to Me oil. Write both your name and your lover's name.

5. Adam and Eve (pink) candle, dressed with Love oil. Write both names again.

6. Suggested Psalms are: 113 (nine times), followed by 45 and 46, and Psalm 140.

7. To a small jar add an object belonging to both you and your lover or mate. Braid them together with three different colored strings, one pink, one white, and one red. Put this into the jar. Add 3 tablespoons of white sugar, a piece of licorice root, ½ teaspoon of damiana, and 1 teaspoon of saw palmetto berries. Shake daily as you concentrate on your mate being faithful. You can also add ½ teaspoon of spikenard herb.

To Obtain Luck in Love

At times it seems difficult to find true love. Many go from one relationship to another. Or you may find yourself in a string of one-date relationships. You need to improve your love life.

1. Chuparosa (red and green) candle, dressed with Compelling and Love Drawing oils. Write your name nine times on paper.

2. Adam and Eve (pink) candle, dressed with Compelling and Love oils mixed. Write your name.

3. Chameleon (red) candle, dressed with Compelling and Love oil. Write your name.

4. Past Luck (yellow and green) candle, dressed with Fast Luck oil. Write your name.

5. Controlling candle, dressed with Fast Luck oil. Write your name. Every day pray the Song of Solomon chapter 8, for a woman, or the Song of Solomon chapter 6, for a man. Finish with Psalm 16 (nine times), to change an unhappy situation to a happy one.

6. The suggested spiritual bath for a woman is made with rose petals, lavender, and cinnamon. For a man the bath should consist of 3 grains of paradise seeds (no more than 3), and 1 teaspoon each of galangal root, damiana, and orris root.

To Obtain Spiritual Strength

At times our faith can waver, the pressure of the world bearing down on our shoulders, making it seem difficult to go on.

1. Twenty-third Psalm candle, dressed with Holy oil. Write your name.

2. King Solomon candle, dressed with King Solomon oil. Write your name.

3. Block Buster (gold and pink) candle, dressed with Holy oil. Again, write your name.

4. Suggested Psalms: 129 to gain spiritual power, 141 to dispel fear, and 115 to increase your faith.

5. A spiritual bath beneficial in this siutation would be made with the Seven Holy Herbs.

To Reconcile with Your Lover or Mate

Separations in relationships are inevitable. No marriages are made in heaven. At times the break up may have had help from an outside source.

1. Adam and Eve (pink) candle, dressed with Come to Me oil. Write your name on top of your lover's name.

2. Come to Me candle, dressed with Come to Me oil. Write both names.

3. Controlling candle, dressed with Compelling oil. Write both names.

4. DUME candle, dressed with Black Art oil. Write your lover's name only.

5. Cross of Caravaca candle, dressed with Compelling oil. Write both your name and your lover's name.

6. Here you pray that your lover will have no peace of mind, no rest, no happiness or joy with others until he

or she is back at your side. Suggested Psalms: 123 for
the return of a lover, Psalm 16 to reconcile, and Psalm
62 to find forgiveness.

7. On a piece of paper write the lover's name in full nine
   times in a cross. Dress an orange household candle with
   Has No Hanna oil. Stick two pins into the candle at
   opposite ends. Place the candle on top of the paper with
   your ex-lover's name. Pray: "It is not the blood of
   (name) I wish to burn, but the heart of (name) I wish to
   turn. Come to me, come to me, that you should love
   only me. May you neither sleep nor rest, nor comfort
   find, until (name) in my arms I ardently bind." Let the
   candle burn until the pins drop. Fold the paper and
   carry it in your shoe.

To Win the Love of Another

It is nice to be in love. It is even nicer to have the one we want.
However, there is a trap in this particular type of work. This
type of ritual can border on black magick, but most people
who are driven by passion and lust want the one they want to
be with, with no thought of the negative results to this particular relationship.

1. Adam and Eve (red) candle, dressed with Love and
   Compelling oils mixed. Write your name and the other
   person's name on paper.

2. Cross of Caravaca candle, dressed with Compelling oil.
   Write both names.

3. Chuparosa (red and green) candle, dressed with Love and Compelling oils mixed. Write both names.

4. Read the Song of Solomon chapter 6 for a man, or the Song of Solomon chapter 8 for a woman.

5. Suggested spiritual bath is the same as given in "To Obtain Luck in Love."

6. On a piece of paper 6 inches by 6 inches square, draw a heart dripping with blood. On the back of the paper write, nine times, your name and the name of the person whose love you want to win, with your name on top of the other's. Stick three pins into the paper as you say: "I pierce your heart with arrows of love." Put ¼ teaspoon of Dragon's Blood resin on the paper. Burn in a fire as you say: "Burn, flame, light this love. Bright as the stars above. Cause (name) heart to beat for me. Light (name) passion to burn for me. Light this love for all to see."

To Keep You on Your Lover's Mind

When separated from the one you love for reasons outside of your control, try this forget-me-not set-up. If you are a man, using this formula, substitute "she" or "her" where appropriate.

1. St. Martha (green) candle, dressed with Jasmine oil. Write your lover's name only.

2. Black Tobacco candle, dressed with Jasmine oil. Write name.

3. Come to Me candle, dressed with Compelling and Come to Me oil mixed. Write your lover's name and your name. Say the following prayer:

I offer this prayer to the charitable spirits for the Guardian Angel of _____, for the Holy Day on which he was born, for the four winds, each of them and their places in which they find. Have him cling to me, love me, and do not let him forget me.

Spirit of the forces, so you can give strength to _____ so he can love me and come to me wherever I am.

Spirit of the illusions, the illusion of _____ be passed on to me. Spirit of despair so that the desperation of _____ be passed on to me. Spirit of splendor and money so that the money he brings home will be put into my hands.

Charitable spirits, here I surrender body, soul, and will of _____. Do not let him sleep, drink, walk, or work without thoughts of me put into _____'s mind, that my name is _____.

Amen.

St. Martha, conquer _____, keep me in his mind.

St. Martha, conquer _____, keep me in his mind.

St. Martha, conquer _____, keep me in his mind.

Amen.

This is the Tobacco prayer, invoking St. Martha's help.

To Gain Cooperation of Others

Things just seem to flow nice and easy when people cooperate with one another, but there are times when it may become necessary to help the cooperation along. Cooperation is a key to successful business deals.

1. Do As I Say candle, dressed with either Bend Over, Do as I Say, or Controlling oil. Write your name eleven times on top of the nine copies of the name of the other person who is to cooperate with you.

2. Controlling candle, dressed with the same oil as the Do As I Say candle. Write your name eleven times, and the other person's name nine times, with your name on top of theirs.

3. King Solomon or High John the Conqueror candle, dressed with the oil by the same name. Again your name is written eleven times on top of the other person's name written nine times.

4. Suggested Psalms are: Psalm 130 (nine times), and 133 (nine times).

5. In a small, wide-mouth jar put a piece of camphor. Take a two-inch piece of vitex (lilac chaste tree, vencedor), and on a piece of paper write the person's name nine times. On top of this name write your name eleven times, and wrap the paper tightly around the vitex. The names must be touching the wood. Tie the paper so that it doesn't unroll from the vitex stick. Put this in the jar

with a piece of High John the Conqueror root. Fill the jar with bourbon whiskey. Pray that you will be able to control and influence the person whose name is tied around the vitex. To work it, you take out the John the Conqueror root from the jar, rub it between the palms, concentrating on the person, and then touch the person. Add some Devil's Shoestring to the jar.

To Draw Back a Strayed Lover

Abandonment—most people fear it happening to them. How many have been in relationships for a long period of time and then one day woke up to find their loved one had just walked out of their life? They were dropped.

1. Intranquil Spirit candle, dressed with Come to Me oil. Write your lover's name nine times on a square of paper. Write your name from one corner to the other corner of the paper, making an X.

2. Black Tobacco candle, dressed with Tobacco oil. Again write the names the same way as for the Intranquil Spirit candle. Use jasmine oil with Tobacco oil.

3. Anima Sola candle, dressed with Come to Me oil. Write the names in the same way again. You can substitute a Guardian Angel. Recite Psalm 123 and prayer to the seven Intranquil Spirits as given in *Helping Yourself With Selected Prayers* (Original Publications, 1988).

4. On a piece of paper, write the person's name nine times in a cross pattern. Place the paper in a clear glass. Add

three tablespoons of white sugar and fill the glass with water. Put the glass on top of a small mirror. Place an open pair of scissors tied in a cross on top of the glass. At the base of the glass place four lodestones or magnets: north, east, south, west, and a magnet on top of the scissors.

To Keep Your Job

In Louisiana there are no job protection laws. Your employer can fire you at any time for whatever reason. To your boss you are only chattel. Whatever the reason is, your pink slip will say either undependable or causing dissension in the work place, or customers complained about the employee's conduct.

1. Steady Work candle, dressed with Steady Work or Success oils. Write your name nine times and your place of employment.

2. St. Joseph candle, dressed with St. Joseph oil or Success oil. Here write your name and place of employment.

3. Success candle, dressed with Success oil. Write your name and place of employment.

4. Psalms 41, 47, and prayer to St. Joseph. While saying the psalms and prayer, shell and eat nine whole pecans. On a 6-inch square of paper, write your name nine times and your place of employment. Mix the pieces of pecan shells with equal parts of passion flower and five-finger grass. You may also add a bit of powdered egg shell to this. This is all wrapped in black-colored

material and bound by wrapping white thread around its whole length to make a "toby" or helping hand. It is important to pray to keep your job while wrapping the white thread around the toby. Hide the toby in your place of employment. As long as it remains in place and is not disturbed, your job is secure. Let someone find it and throw it out with the garbage, and you may soon find yourself out of work.

Reverse a Curse to Known and Unknown Enemies

There are times in life when you seem to be up against difficult situations. Every time you turn around you bump into a wall. Every time you seem to get ahead, you are knocked back down.

1. St. Expedite candle, dressed with St. Expedite oil. Write your name nine times.

2. Reversible (white and black) candle, dressed with Dragon Blood oil.

3. Uncrossing (purple) candle, dressed with Uncrossing oil. Write your name nine times.

4. Reversible (red and black) candle, dressed with Dragon Blood oil.

5. Uncrossing (white) dressed with Uncrossing oil.

6. Reversible (green and black) candle, dressed with Dragon Blood oil.

7. Fast Luck (seven-color) candle, dressed with Fast Luck and Success mixed. Write your name nine times.

8. On each Reversible candle you will write your name in the wax at the top of the candle. On paper you will write: "Evil and harm that is sent to me returns to its source three times three."

9. Psalms 53, 54, 55, and 100 (nine times), 59 (three times), and 65 (nine times). Take an Uncrossing or Jinx Remover bath. Add a tea made from hydrangea, blessed thistle, rue, vetivert, galangal, and perfume this spiritual bath with Kolonia 1800.

To Get a Loan

When your credit is shaky and you need some extra cash, it is quite possible that some loan companies will turn you down.

1. Money Release candle, dressed with Money Release oil or Money Drawing oil. Write your name and amount of loan you are applying for.

2. Do As I Say candle, dressed with Do as I Say oil or Compelling, Power, High John, or King Solomon oil. Write your name eleven times. Write the name of the person who will okay the loan nine times. Your name should cover the other person's name.

3. Reversible (green and black) candle, dressed with Dragon Blood oil. Write your name in the green wax at the top and on paper write the person's name nine times and the amount of the loan after their name.

4. Psalms 4 and 41, repeated three times. Take a spiritual bath made with nutmeg, yellow dock root, and sassafras. Allow the bath water to air dry on your skin. Smudge your body with incense mixed with allspice, rue, and benzoin.

Break Up a Negative Condition in the Home

After the stress and strain of working outside the home, fighting the rush hour traffic, it is not an enjoyable experience to come home to a situation where there is a lot of stress and confusion. Are those who should be living together in harmony, at war? Does your mate take his or her frustrations out on you when he or she gets home from work?

1. Peaceful Home (blue and white) candle, dressed with Peace oil. Write the name of person(s) creating the disturbance nine times.

2. Make Your Wish or Buda (pink) candle, dress with Love oil. Write the person's name.

3. Peace candle, dressed with Peace oil. Write the name of the person(s) creating the disturbance.

4. Psalms 1 and 133, 96 and 97. Burn every three days in incense a mixture of dried, chopped garlic, brown sugar, and benzoin. Sprinkle a mixture of Florida water and rose cologne about the home.

For Protection from Enemies

It doesn't matter how good a person you can be. No one goes through life without making an enemy here and there. Some enemies can be vicious and want some kind of revenge, whether the reason is real or imaginary.

1. Protection candle, dressed with Protection oil. Write your name nine times.

2. Block Buster (dark red and black) candle, dressed with Dragon Blood oil. Write your name the same as for a reversible.

3. Guardian Angel candle, dressed with Holy oil. Write your name nine times. Use the prayer to the Guardian Angel. Psalms 7, 22, and 44.

4. The Block Buster candle can be substituted by a St. Michael (red) or a Just Judge (white). Use the prayer to St. Michael or Just Judge prayer if you are using the candle.

Spiritual bath: a mixture of ½ cup epsom salt, I cup table or sea salt, ¼ cup baking soda, 1 cup apple cider vinegar, and 1 cup of yellow Chinese wash. You may also use Protection from Harm or Protection from Enemies bath and floor wash.

To Gain Luck in Gambling

Some people just seem to be lucky at games of chance. Gambling in one form or another has been around for centuries. Warning! Gambling can cause you some serious financial problems and keep you broke, but then again, I have seen people able to buy the things needed for their home and family with money won at gambling.

1. Hunchback candle, dressed with a Gambling oil such as Has No Hanna, Lucky Slots, Lucky Dog. Write your name nine times.

2. Fast Luck (seven colors) candle, dressed with a Gambling oil. Write your name.

3. If you are playing bingo, use a Bingo candle; if you are going to the casino, use a Casino/Gamblers candle; for the racetrack, use a One Drop of Luck candle or a Lucky Horseshoe candle; if you play cards, a Helping Hand candle. Dress the candle with your Gambling oil, and write your name nine times.

4. Psalms 4 (three times), 76, and 65. Take a spiritual bath made with seven holy herbs. Wear Jockey Club cologne.

5. Carry a Gambling mojo/gris-gris with you while you are gambling. When not gambling keep it near the candles. To make this yourself, in a red flannel bag put a tonka bean, nutmeg, High John root, a piece of Dragon's Blood reed wrapped in a dollar bill, a buckeye, and red clover.

To Remove Evil from Your Path

Sometimes the very people we trust seem to send out negative thoughts about the plans and projects we may be engaged in. We all encounter those who seem to be in agreement with our plans as we discuss our lives with them, but at the same time they are praying that we fail in our endeavor. This is a case where you can be hexing yourself with your own mouth by talking too much.

1. Uncrossing (purple) candle, dress with Uncrossing oil. Write your name nine times.

2. Road Opener candle, dressed with Road Opener oil. Write your name.

3. Go Away Evil (purple and black) candle, dressed with Jinx Removing oil. Write your name.

4. Success candle, dressed with Success oil. Write your name and desire.

5. Guardian Angel candle, dressed with Protection oil. Write your name. Psalms 65 and 57. You may also add Psalm 98.

6. Take a spiritual bath with slippery elm, vetivert, and hyssop. A female should also add parsley flakes sweetened with honey. A man should add galangal, nutmeg, and sweetened honey.

To Get a Job

With the overpopulation problems and people always moving to greener pastures, it can be difficult to find a good job. At times it may be necessary to find a second job to supplement your income.

1. Job candle, dressed with Steady Work oil or Job oil. Write your name and desire.

2. St. Joseph candle, dressed with St. Joseph oil. Write your name.

3. Road Opener candle, dressed with Road Opener oil. Write your name and desire. Psalms 4 and 41 (three times), and the prayer to St. Joseph.

4. Take a spiritual bath made with pecan shells, red clover, and nutmeg. Wear Interview oil. Carry a St. Joseph prayer card with you in your wallet or purse.

To Break Up a Love Affair

This is the classic petition. It may not be just a friend trying to come between you and your lover or fiancée; I have seen many mothers use this on their own children.

1. Break Up (black) candle, dressed with Break Up or Black Art oils. Write the names of the two lovers nine times.

2. Negative green (to symbolize jealousy) candle, dressed with Double Cross oil. Write both names, or the name of the person you want to be seen as jealous in the relationship.

3. Get Away candle, dressed with Break Up or Black Art oils. Write both names.

4. A brown candle, dressed with Confusion oil. Write both names.

5. Negative red (to symbolize arguments) candle, dressed with Black Art or Confusion oils. Write both names. Psalm 3 (nine times) and Psalm 70.

6. Some people may even place the names inside a lemon. You would cut a slit lengthwise down the lemon, sprinkle Get Away powder on the names, and then put the paper in the slit. Close the slit with nine pins and wrap the lemon with black thread. Throw the lemon in a vacant lot to dry and rot in the sun.

To Eliminate a Rival

To compete with another who desires the same person as you do can bring out very negative emotions such as jealousy, insecurity, and even hatred. There are some individuals in the world who prefer only to be romantically involved with married people. If you know the name of your rival, try this one.

1. Adam and Eve (red) candle, dressed with Strong Love, Compelling, or Come to Me oil. Write your name and the name of the person you desire.

2. St. Anthony (orange) candle, dressed with St. Anthony oil. Write your name and the person's name whom you desire.

3. St. Helen (pink) candle, dressed with the same oil as the Adam and Eve candle.

4. A gray candle, dressed with Confusion oil. Write the rival's name.

5. DUME candle, dressed with Black Art oil. Write the rival's name. Read or recite Psalms 70, 93 and 55 while praying for your rival's failure in interfering.

6. Call your lover's name three times, then pray Psalm 138, 139, and, for a woman, the Song of Solomon chapter 8. For a man, the Song of Solomon chapter 6.

7. Make and use the spiritual bath as given in "To Obtain Luck in Love." To this spiritual bath add ¼ cup of Adam and Eve bath and floor wash.

To Eliminate a Rival for Your Job

Climbing the ladder of success in any business or corporation has its own dangers to be aware of. In life you have to fight to get what you want. Then, once you have it, you have to fight to keep it. There will always be someone on the sidelines waiting to take away from you what you have. To help your climb to the top, work with this for future promotions.

1. Job candle, dressed with Job, Steady Work, Success oils. Write your name and the job position you want.

2. St. Peter candle, dressed with Success oil. Write your name and the job position you want.

3. St. Michael (purple) candle, dressed with St. Michael, Success, or John the Conqueror oils. Write your name and the job position you want.

4. A gray candle, dressed with Confusion oil. Write your rival's name.

5 DUME candle, dressed with Black Art oil. Write your rival's name.

6. Psalms 4 and 41 (nine times), 93 (three times). Use the novena prayer to St. Peter, asking St. Michael to help defend your position. Use a spiritual bath made with ¼ cup of John the Conqueror bath and floor wash, ½ cup of epsom salt, ½ cup of table or sea salt, ¼ cup of baking soda, 1 cup of apple cider vinegar. Allow bath to air dry on your skin. Fumigate/smoke your body with allspice mixed with John the Conqueror incense.

To Improve Your Business

All businesses have their slow periods as well as their busiest seasons. For the slow days, or if you are trying to get started in your business:

1. Better Business candle, dressed with Jinx Removing and Success oils combined. Write the name of the business.

2. St. Martin of Tours (in Spanish he is known as St. Martin Caballero). You may substitute a Pancho Villa candle, dressed with Success or Steady Work oils. Write the name of the business.

3. Steady Work candle, dressed with Steady Work and Success oils combined. Write the name of the business.

4. Psalms 5, 14, and 65. Add to the mop water a tea made from red clover, honeysuckle, cinnamon, and yellow dock. Mop from the front entrance, coming into the place. Burn an incense made with cinnamon, myrrh, and frankincense.

If Your Business Has Been Jinxed or Hoodooed

It is possible to come to work one morning and find powders or strange objects placed at your business door. When there are too many businesses of the same type, too close together in the same area, a proprietor may feel the need to eliminate the competition in some way. He or she may be tempted to put a jinx on your business. In order to survive, and not become a victim, you could take these steps:

1. Uncrossing (purple) dressed with Uncrossing oil. Write the name of the business.

2. High John the Conqueror (3 color) candle, dressed with John the Conqueror oil. Write the name of the business.

3. Block Buster (dark red and black) candle, dressed with Dragon Blood oil. Write the name of the business.

4. St. Peter candle, dressed with St. Peter oil. Write the name of the business.

5. Go Away Evil candle, dressed with Uncrossing oil. Write the name of the business.

6. Psalm 5 (three times), 59, and 93.

To Attract Success

It is natural to want to be successful in all of our undertakings. Success comes with hard work and perseverance. Each time you fall, you must get back up again.

1. Cross of Caravaca candle, dressed with Success oil. Add a tonka bean in the candle wax. Write your name and

the project for which you want success. For example, if you want success in sports, write your name and the word "sports."

2. Success candle, dressed with Success oil. Write your name and a word describing the area of success desired.

3. Road Opener candle, dressed with Road Opener oil. Write your name as for the other candles.

4. Psalms suggested are 57, 65, and 98. Take a spiritual bath with red clover, John the Conqueror root, and five-finger grass. Add to this tea High John the Conqueror bath and floor wash.

To Keep the Law Away

Some people seem to be constantly harassed by the police. Every time they get behind the wheel of a car, they are stopped for some reason. Then there are those whose occupations are a bit illegal.

1. Law Stay Away candle, dressed with Law Stay Away oil. Write your name and the initials of your city's police department.

2. Get Away candle, dress with Uncrossing oil. Write your name and the initials of the police department of your city.

3. Guardian Angel candle, dressed with Power oil. Write your name and the initials of police department.

4. Keep a St. Michael prayer card with you in your wallet or purse. Recite Psalms 9 and 53, and finish with Psalm 16 nine times. Make a spiritual bath with fenugreek seeds, nutmeg, galangal, and cascara sagrada. Add ¼ cup of Jinx Removing bath and floor wash, ½ cup of epsom salt, ½ cup of table or sea salt, ¼ cup of baking soda, and 1 cup of apple cider vinegar.

To Overcome Fear

Sometimes fear can be difficult to shake off when it gets hold of you. Then there are those people who get a thrill from putting fear and superstition in your mind.

1. Controlling candle, dressed with Controlling oil. Write your name nine times.

2. St. Dymphna candle, dressed with Peace oil. Write your name nine times.

3. Guardian Angel candle, dressed with Peace oil. Write your name three times.

4. Psalms 11, 31, and 141.

5. Take an Uncrossing spiritual bath made with sweet basil, boneset, elder, and bay leaves. To this tea add ¼ cup of John the Conqueror bath and floor wash. Immerse yourself three times in the water, and soak twenty minutes. Take this spiritual bath every three days until you have taken twenty-eight baths. Carry a mojo/gris-gris made with herbs for courage. This gris/gris must also contain a stone for courage such as

agate, amethyst, aquamarine, bloodstone, carnelian, diamond, lapis lazuli, sardonyx, tiger's eye, red tourmaline, or turquoise.

To Protect Your Money From Being Hoodooed or Jinxed

Many times a person may think you have more money than you do in reality. If you have lent money to another and are having financial problems later, the person you have loaned the money to has jinxed your money supply. Even relatives can be jealous of your financial prosperity.

1. Ajo Macho candle, dressed with Fast Luck oil. Write your name and the word "finances."

2. Money House candle, dressed with protection oil. Write your name and the word "finances."

3. Reversible (green and black) candle, dressed with Dragon Blood oil. Write your name and the word "finances."

4. Jinx Remover (three-color) candle, dressed with Jinx Remover oil. Write your name and and the word "finances."

5. Protection candle, dressed with Protection oil. Write your name and the word "finances."

6. Carry a toe of garlic in your Money Drawing gris-gris/mojo. Do not try to impress others with your prosperity; this can provoke unnecessary jealousy.

To Cause Another to Perjure Themselves in Court

At a time when you can confuse another person's testimony against you in court, you may have a better chance of winning the case.

1. Court Case (brown) candle, dressed with Confusion oil. Sprinkle a bit of five-finger grass and brown mustard seeds in the candle. Write the person's name nine times and the word "contradict."

2. Negative White (to symbolize an untruth) candle, dressed with Confusion oil. Write the person's name and the word "contradict."

3. DUME candle, dressed with Confusion oil. Write the person's name. On each paper containing the person's name sprinkle a bit of five-finger grass.

4. Psalms 70 and 63 nine times each.

To Pressure Your Attorney to Settle Your Case

Have you been involved in an accident? Do you have a lawsuit in the courts? If it seems that your attorney is not doing anything to get your case settled as quickly as possible, try this to fan the flames.

1. St. Expedite candle, dressed with St. Expedite oil. Write your name eleven times, and the attorney's name nine times. Your name should cover the attorney's name.

2. King Solomon candle, dressed with King Solomon oil. Your name should cover the attorney's name.

3. Success candle, dressed with Success oil. Again your name should cover the attorney's name.

4. Psalms 130, 133 and 122. Each time before you visit the attorney in person, take a spiritual bath made with Seven Holy Herbs and ½ teaspoon of nutmeg. Let the bath water air dry on your skin. Anoint your pulse points with High John the Conqueror oil.

To Get Another to Speak Their Mind

When you know that something is bothering another it can be very frustrating to get them to open up. At times in any relationship it is good to have some sort of reassurance as to where we are standing with the other.

1. High John the Conqueror candle, dressed with High John oil. Write the person's name nine times.

2. Yellow (seven-day plain glass) candle, dressed with Mind oil. Write the person's name.

3. Peace candle, dressed with Peace oil. Write the person's name.

4. In each of the candles, sprinkle a bit of five-finger grass, and on each piece of paper where the person's name is written place a bit of five-finger grass.

5. Psalm 117 (repeated thirty-five times).

To Get a Divorce

Not all marriages are made in heaven. Some people marry for reasons other than love. When you have gotten what you wanted out of the marriage and it's time to move on to greener pastures, you may have a problem in getting the divorce.

1. Just Judge (red) candle, dressed with Rose oil. Write your name and the word "divorced."

2. Court Case (brown) candle, dressed with Confusion oil. Write your mate's name and the word "divorced."

3. Success candle, dressed with Success oil. Write your name and the word "divorced."

4. Psalm 3 nine times, 35 and 36. Three days before the court hearing take a spiritual bath made with sascara sagrada, galangal, and nutmeg, to which is added ⅓ bottle of Devil's Shoestring bath and floor wash.

To Keep Your Mate Faithful

When both husband and wife work it can put a strain on any relationship, especially if one works nights and the other days. Even if this is not the case and you suspect your mate of cheating:

1. St. Martha candle, dressed with St. Martha oil. Write your name and lover's name nine times each.

2. Love Drawing candle, dressed with Spikenard oil. Write your name and lover's name.

3. Adam and Eve (red) candle, dressed with Adam and Eve, Lovers, Spikenard, and Come to Me oils. Write your name and your lover's. Use the prayer to St. Martha and Psalms 113, 139, and 140.

4. Some people will put a picture of their beloved in a jar and cover the picture with hyssop and rose petals. Daily they shake the jar and they talk sweet, sweet, sweet to the beloved as they pray the St. Martha prayer.

5. Take a soiled piece of your lover's clothing (as an object link) and wear it inside of your underwear for seven days. On the eighth day, tie the object link of your lover to an object of yours with red thread. Place it in a jar with three teaspoons of sugar, spikenard, damiana, and licorice root. Top the jar and seal it with wax.

To Get Your Job Back

Beware if there is a clique going on at your place of employment. If you are not a part of the clique, you can be a target, catching the blame for another's mistakes. At times a supervisor will lie to cause the one they don't like to lose their job. There is a remedy for losing your job through falsehood.

1. Job candle, dressed with Job oil. Write your name and place of work.

2. High John the Conqueror (purple) candle, dressed with oil of same name. Write your name and place of work.

3. St. Anthony (green) candle, dressed with St. Anthony oil. Write your name and workplace. Use the prayer to St. Anthony and Psalms 41, 42, 43.

4. Write your name and place of employment on a piece of paper. Wrap this around a whole pecan with orange,

yellow, and green colored string. Take seven job's tears, some red clover, and a lodestone. Put everything in a red flannel bag. Place the bag in front of the John the Conqueror candle. Write your boss' name on a piece of paper and place it in a clear glass. Put three tablespoons of white sugar on top of the paper and fill the glass with water. Set this glass in the center of a plate (preferably white) and surround the glass with brown sugar. On either side of the glass of water light a purple and an orange household candle. On these candles write your name and your boss' name. Naturally the household candles will be held upright by the brown sugar. The two household candles are lit only during your prayer time, then extinguished afterward.

To Uncover the Truth

From time to time we all encounter situations where we are filled with doubt in our minds. Then again, there are those who will deliberately lie about the causes of a problem, perhaps to protect themselves from the guilt of wrongdoing.

1. Sacred Heart of Jesus (white) candle, dressed with Holy or Anointing oil. Your name is written nine tines.

2. Blue colored plain glass candle, dressed with Holy or Anointing oil. Again write your name.

3. Twenty-third Psalm (white) candle, dressed with Holy or Anointing oil. Write your name.

By doing this setup, the truth can come to you through a dream or by confession. Pray about the subject that you wish the truth to be revealed for.

Suggested Psalms are 117 (repeated 35 times), and 23 (seven times). Take a spiritual bath made with the Seven Holy Herbs to which is added ½ cup epsom salt, 1I cup table or sea salt, ¼ cup baking soda, 1 cup apple cider vinegar, ¼ cup white uncrossing bath and floor wash or coconut bath and floor wash. The apple cider vinegar helps to prevent the salts from drying your skin, plus it is a good tonic for the skin.

To Improve Studies in School

As an adult, working and going to college can be tough. I know this firsthand because I was working while I went to nursing school. At times it can be difficult for students in elementary, middle, and high school to make good grades. As it is now in some areas, if you do not pass the exit exam you will not graduate from high school, even if you did make good grades.

1. Cross of Caravaca candle, dressed with Success oil. Write your name. Add one tonka bean to the Cross of Caravaca candle.

2. High John the Conqueror (purple) candle, dressed with John the Conqueror oil. Add a bit of red clover.

3. Blue candle in plain glass, dressed with Success oil. To this candle add a bit of sage and rosemary. While studying, burn ¼ teaspoon of alum mixed with 1 teaspoon of any powdered incense.

4. If you are still a tad nervous about an upcoming exam, you may add a Success candle dressed with Success oil, and include some red clover, sage, and rosemary. You may also use an orange Controlling candle dressed with Controlling oil. Add the same herbs as the Success candle.

5. Suggested Psalms are 19, 119, verses 9–16 of both Psalms. For passing exams use Psalm 134.

To Gain Peace of Mind

Peace of mind is a blessing. For the mother hens who always worry, it does not come easy. When routines are suddenly broken and we do not know where our loved ones are, peace of mind seems to vanish.

1. St. Dymphna candle, dressed with Peace oil. Write your name nine times.

2. Peace candle, dressed with Peace oil. Again write your name.

3. Guardian Angel candle, dressed with Peace oil. Write your name.

4. Psalms 119, verses 49–56, 15 and 16. Take a spiritual bath using ¼ cup blue condition, 1 cup epsom salt, 1 cup table or sea salt, 1 cup baking soda, and 1 cup of apple cider vinegar. Sit twenty minutes in a half-filled tub.

To Overcome Troublesome Neighbors

What a nightmare living next door to people who are always fussing and fighting. Do you have a neighbor who seems to drop by at the most inconvenient times? How about the nosy neighbor?

1. Get Away candle, dressed with Black Art oil. Write the neighbor's name and the word "farewell."

2. Go Away Evil candle, dressed with Black Art oil. Write the neighbor's name and the word "farewell."

3. Run Devil Run candle, dressed with Run Devil Run or Black Art oil. Write the neighbor's name and the word "farewell."

4. Psalms 74, 101, and 109. Mix powdered mud dauber's nest with Get Away powder and throw it at the neighbor's door. Sprinkle a bit of this mixture on the neighbor's name that is placed under each candle.

To Cause Someone to Move Out of a House

1. Use the same candle setup as above. Take any kind of onion: use a flat onion for a male and a pointed onion for a female. Cut a plug out of the center of the onion. Write the person's name in a crisscross, sprinkle a bit of Get Away powder on the paper and tightly wad the paper. This is stuffed into the hole made in the onion. Put the plug back in its place and tightly wrap the onion in red cloth. Wait until the person leaves the

house. Roll the onion across the person's path to the door, saying, "Get out, go away," seven times. Hide the onion where the person will come in contact with it often. They will become so uncomfortable in time that they will move out. After they are gone, throw the onion in the river.

To Gain Power over Another

Power can be a deadly word. It is the uncontrolled desire to have power over others that can create problems in our own lives. Many people will stop at nothing to get it. Though it is possible to get power over another, keeping it is another thing.

1. King Solomon candle, dressed with King Solomon oil. Write your name eleven times over the other person's name written nine times.

2. Controlling candle, dressed with Controlling oil. Write your name over the other's name.

3. High John the Conqueror candle, dressed with John the Conqueror oil. Write your name over the other's name.

4. Do As I Say candle, dressed with Controlling oil. Write your name over the other's name.

5. Guardian Angel candle, dressed with Peace oil. Write the name of the person whom you want to control. Place a glass of water with the person's name written nine times inside the glass of water with three tablespoons of white sugar.

6. Repeat Psalms 130 and 133 nine times each. Pray to the person's guardian angel to sweeten the person toward your influence. Use the "Prayer to the Spirit of Desperation."

In the hour of grief of my soul, oppressed with uncertainty, I invoke with all the strength and good will of my spirit, that you possess the five senses of, and let him/her dedicate his/her faith, love, and faithfulness only to me.

Come, Spirit of Desperation, hear my plea which I implore in the name of the Father, Son, and Holy Spirit.

Amen.

"The Prayer to the Spirit of Desperation" is taken from the book *Helping Yourself With Selected Prayers* by Original Publications. If your supplier does not have a copy of this book, contact the publisher. Their address and phone number is listed on page 223. It is given here as an example of how these prayers can be used in folk magick.

To Gain Power Over Another (Bend Over Spell)

This spell is also in used combination with the candle set up to gain Power Over Another.

1. On a white jumbo candle, write the name of the person whom you want to influence. A jumbo candle is ½ inch in diameter, and 9 inches tall, the largest of the household stick candles. A white taper candle will work just as

well, but the jumbo is traditional. Pour a small amount of Bend Over oil, also known as essence of Bend Over, into the palm of your hand. The candle is anointed by twisting it through your hand. This is symbolic of turning the person's mind to your will. The candle is then rolled through a powder made of a mixture of salt, camphor, asafoetida, and powdered solomon seal root. Light the candle and allow it to burn to the end. On the third night the powder mixture must be thrown across the path where the one to be ruled will walk.

To Destroy Someone's Power Over Another

It can be very frustrating being involved in a relationship when your mate constantly jumps up, dropping what he or she is doing with you, at the beck and call of another.

1. Jinx Removing (black) candle, dressed with Confusion or Black Art oil. Write the name of the person who is in control nine times and the word "powerless."

2. Controlling candle, dressed with Double Cross oil. Write the name of the controlling person nine times and the word "powerless."

3. A gray candle, dressed with Double Cross oil. Write the name of the controlling person.

4. DUME candle, dressed with Black Art oil. Write both names, the one who controls and the one being controlled.

5. Guardian Angel candle, dressed with Frankincense oil. Write the name of the one controlled.

6. Psalms 117 (three times), 70, 101, and 109.

To Heal an Unhappy Marriage

No marriage is made in heaven. All relationships begin to change within the first five to seven years of togetherness. For a marriage to survive past seven years both parties must change and mature together as the relationship changes. If not, divorce is inevitable.

1. Adam and Eve (red) candle, dressed with Adam and Eve oil. Write both husband and wife's name.

2. St. Anthony (orange) candle, dressed with orange or Marriage oil. Again write both names.

3. Gold candle, dressed with Attraction oil. Write both names.

4. Psalms 45, 469 139, and 140. Also use the prayer to St. Anthony.

5. The wife takes a dirty dishrag and sleeps with it under her pillow. After she and her husband have intercourse, she will wipe her husband and herself with it. She will then tie three knots in the dishrag the next morning, without her husband knowing it, and keep the dishrag under the mattress of the bed.

6. Soak in Evangeline cologne some spikenard, rose petals, and lavender. Light a red household candle and pray,

invoking St. Helen of Jerusalem to assist in keeping
your marriage together. Let the candle burn down only
one-third of its length. Repeat on two more days. Some
will place the candle in the center of a large bowl with
the cologne and herbs around the candle as they make
the three-day prayer. Each time you change the bed
sheets, sprinkle them with the cologne.

To Get Married

"Always a bridesmaid and never a bride," the saying goes.
When fifteen- and sixteen-year-old girls have their mind set on
marriage, one thing is certain: it is not because of love. The
motive is because they want to get out of their parents' home.
Marriage has always been the easy way to do this and avoid a
scandal. On the other hand, when parents are pushing for
their daughter to marry at that young age, it is because they
(the parents) want the daughter out of the house. Getting
pregnant today will not guarantee that the child's father will do
the right thing by marrying the mother to save her from the
disgrace of being an unwed mother.

1. St. Anthony (orange) candle, dressed with orange or
   Marriage oil. Write your name and the name of the one
   you want to marry nine times on paper.

2. Adam and Eve (pink) candle, dressed with Love oil.
   Write both your names.

3. Chuparosa (red and green) candle, dressed with Love
   oil. Again write both of your names.

4. St. Martha (green) candle, dressed with St. Martha oil. Write both of your names. (Used by women only.)

5. Reversible (red and black) candle, dressed with Reversible oil. Write the initials of both of your names in the red wax.

6. Men should use a St. Joseph candle in place of the St. Martha used by women. Call your beloved's name three times, then say Psalm 138, and 139, and the Song of Solomon chapter 6 for men or the Song of Solomon chapter 8 for women. Use the prayer to both saints. Use a spiritual bath made with yarrow.

To Gain Prosperity

It has been said that if a business' profits increase by ten percent each year, the business is prospering. When you are able to save or earn ten percent more each year in your savings account, then you are prospering. Anything less than this and you are only surviving on the sea of life. You can use the seven-day, plain glass vigil lights for this ritual.

1. Purple colored candle, dressed with Money Drawing and Success oil. Write your name nine times.

2. Green colored candle, dressed with Money Drawing and Fast Luck oil. Write your name nine times.

3. Orange colored candle, dressed with Lodestone and Money Drawing oils.

4. Gold colored candle, dressed with Lodestone and Success oils. Again write your name nine times each for both the orange- and gold-colored, seven-day vigils.

5. White colored candle, dressed with Frankincense oil. Write your name nine times.

6. Psalms 41, 62, 57, and 65.

7. Take a spiritual bath using green-colored Chinese wash and salt mixture of ½ cup, epsom salt, ½ cup of table or sea. salt, ¼ cup baking soda, 1 cup of apple cider vinegar, and ½ cup Chinese wash. Make a tea using 1 tablespoon each of yellow dock, red clover, rue, sassafras, and five-finger grass. Make 1 gallon of this tea and use 1 cup only per bath. One gallon will give you sixteen baths.

8. If you have a mojo/gris-gris for Money Drawing, place it between the green and orange candles. Leave it there until the candles burn themselves out. This will freshen the gris-gris.

To Keep Money in the Home

When the money is leaving as fast as it is coming in, it appears as though you will never get ahead. Once you get behind with your bills, it can be difficult to catch up.

1. House Blessing candle, dressed with Fast Luck and Money Drawing oils. Write your name.

2. Money Drawing candle, dressed with Fast Luck and Money Drawing oils. Write your name.

3. Seven-Color Fast Luck candle, dressed with Fast Luck and Success oils. Write your name.

4. Psalms 78 and 79. Burn garlic peel on the stove. Sprinkle the house with a tea made from herbs associated with money and add to the tea about 1 ounce of Hoyt's cologne. Do not mop your house with too much ammonia, it will put away your good luck, along with the bad luck. Three tablespoons of ammonia in the mop water once every six months is sufficient. Most practitioners will not tell you this about ammonia because they know that when the bad luck comes, you will be running to them with your money to do a ritual to change the bad luck to good.

To Calm Another's Anger

It can be a bit difficult to get someone to work with us on anything while they are angry, and even harder to reconcile with a mate when they are angry and you two are separated.

1. St. Dymphna candle, dressed with Peace oil. Write the name of the one who is angry.

2. Pink candle in plain glass, dressed with Lodestone oil. Write your name and the other person's name.

3. Guardian Angel candle, dressed with Lodestone oil. Write the name of the person who is angry.

4. Psalms 85, 133, and 138. Daily burn in incense a piece of paper which has the name of the angry person written three times. As you prepare the incense, mix

1 teaspoon of passion flower and ¼ teaspoon of brown sugar. It is best to use a spiritual incense such as Adam and Eve or High John the Conqueror. One tablespoon of the incense blended with the passion flower and brown sugar is sufficient per day. Write the name of the angry person on another piece of paper and put in into a glass. Add three tablespoons of white sugar and 1 teaspoon of honey on the paper with the name. Fill the glass with water and place the glass between the pink candle and the Guardian Angel candle.

To Postpone a Court Case

Sometimes when a trial is postponed four times, it becomes lost in the system and never comes back to trial. The problem is that the charges are still hanging over the person's head.

1. Brown Court Case candle, dressed with Confusion oil. Write the name of the case.

2. Gold Candle in plain glass, dressed with Confusion oil. Write the name of the case.

3. DUME candle, dressed with Black Art oil. Write the name of the case.

4. Psalms 63 and 70 (nine times each).

5. Write the presiding judge's name on a piece of paper. Melt down a black hexing candle and place the paper with the judge's name on this soft wax. Sprinkle the paper with Get Away powder. Mold the wax and paper

into a ball. Let the ball harden and hide it in a dark place until the eve of the trial. Place the wax ball in a pot of water and turn it throughout the night, praying that the judge will take ill and not be able to hold court that day.

To Sell Your Home or Business

It can be a problem when you want to move to another state or to another part of the city, and in order to do it, you must sell your house or business. Many times a home will stay on the market for months before any prospects look at the house.

1. A pink seven-day vigil candle in plain glass for St. Philomena. Dress it with Frankincense and Lodestone oils. Write the name of the business or the house's address and the word "Sold."

2. Money Drawing (gold and green) candle, dressed with Money and Lodestone oil. Write the name of the business or the house's address and the word "Sold."

3. Gold seven-day vigil in plain glass, dressed with Success and Lodestone oils. Write the name of the business or the house's address and the word "Sold."

4. Psalms 82, 65, 62, 98. Make a tea using the following: 1 ½ oz. of cinnamon, 1 ½ oz. of brown sugar, 1 ½ oz. of nutmeg, 1½ oz. of yellow dock root. Use this tea as a floor scrubbing water. Take a shoot glass full of whiskey and sprinkle it into all four corners of the room.

To Cause Jealousy in Another

There is a saying that if a person is not jealous, they don't love you, but jealousy can be a dangerous emotion; if it gets out of hand jealousy can lead to physical violence.

1. A Negative green candle, dressed with Black Art and Double Cross oils. Write the name of the person you want to make jealous and write the word "jealous."

2. Brown seven-day vigil candle, dressed with Confusion oil. Write the person's name and the word "jealous."

3. A Negative green candle, dressed with Black Art and Confusion oils. Write the person's name and the word "jealous."

4. Psalm 63 (nine times). Write the person's name five times on a piece of paper and draw a heart around the names. Using three pins, attach the piece of dirty clothing belonging to the person to the paper with his or her name. Put this into a jar with some graveyard dirt, brown/black mustard seeds, rose petals, and hyssop. Shake the jar as you pray. When finished, place the jar in front of the brown candle, leaving it there until the candle is burned out. Keep the jar in a dark place.

To Protect Against Miscarriage

The first three months of pregnancy are said to be the most dangerous. There are women who decide to try for a baby even when their doctors think it is not in the best interest for the mother's health.

1. St. Raymond Nonnatus candle, dressed with Frankincense oil. Write your name nine times.

2. Blue, white, and red, Victory candle, dressed with Health oil. Write your name.

3. Health candle, dressed with Health and Frankincense oils. Write your name.

4. Psalms 102, 103, 128, and 1.

CANDLE ANOINTING OILS

Most spiritual supply houses carry different types of oils (one supply house has compiled a book containing over 550 oils), but may not have the particular brands or names of oils listed here. To simplify your selection, oils are listed by their category of use. If you cannot find an oil by a particular name, then substitute for it another oil that falls within the same category.

Attraction Oils

Anointing
Attraction
Candle
Consecration
Drawing
Dressing
Exodus
Frankincense or Olibanum
Geranium
Glow of Attraction
Hi-Altar
Hindu
Honeysuckle
Incense
Indian Guide
Invocation
Irresistible
Jacinthe
Lodestone, aka Lucky
   Lodestone
Lotus
Magnet
Mint
Van Van, aka New Orleans
   Van Van
Orris
Olive
Spearmint
Spirit's Guide
Wisteria

Dream and Meditation Oils

Beneficial Dream
Five Circles
Heather
Indian Guide
Lilac
Lily

Magnolia
Meditation
Rama Dream
Saffron
Spirit Guide

Gambling Oils

Carnation
Easy Life
Gambler's Luck
Has No Hanna,
   aka Has No Harra
Jockey Club
Lady Luck
Lucky Bingo
Lucky Dog

Lucky Hand
Lucky Slots
Lucky Win
Narcisse or Narcissus
3 Jacks and a King, same
   as 3 Knaves and a King
Number 20 or Special #20
3 Jacks and a Queen
Winner's Circle

Happiness Oils

All Saints
Bergamot
Blessing
Five-finger Grass
Heliotrope
Lavender

Lemon or Lemon Grass
Naomi
Nine Mystery
Violet
White Rose

Healing Oils

Healing
Heliotrope
Mint

Olive
Peppermint
Snake

Hexing or Jinxing Oils

African Ju Ju
Babel
Bat's Blood
Black Art
Black Cat
Cactus
Citronella
Confusion
Crossing
Devil
Flying Devil
Four Thieves Vinegar
Henbane
Inflammatory Confusion
Jezabel (to be used only
  by a woman)
Jinx
Job Breaker
Ju Ju
Love Breaker, aka Break Up
Midnight Ritual
Mimosa
Mummy
Patchouli
Separation
Sumbul
War
XX Double Cross, same
  as Double Cross

Holy or Spiritual Oils

Altar
Anointing
Balsam
Benzoin
Bible
Blessing
Candle
Cassia
Divine
Exodus
Frankincense
Myrrh
Nine Mystery
Obeah
Occult Ceremony
Olive
Rue
Saffron
Sandalwood
Seven Powers, aka Seven
  African Powers
Special Favor

Holy or Spiritual Oils (cont'd)

Temple

Ten Commandments

Trinity

Van Van

Voodoo Night, aka Voodoo

Love Oils

Adam and Eve

Almond

Angel

Arabian Nights

Cinnamon

Cleo may

Cleopatra

Clove

Come to Me

Coriander

Caliph's Beloved

Dixie Love

Fire of Love

Flame of Desire

Flames of Passion

Glow of Attraction

Has No Hanna

Irresistible

Isis

Jasmine

Lotus

Loveage

Lovers

Luv Luv Luv

Lyang Lyang

Mandrake

Man Trap

Marriage

Myrtle

Orange

Orris

Passion

Patchouli

Queen of Sheba

Q Oil

Rose

Seven Drops of Love

Seventh Heaven

Squint Drops, aka Squint

Stay Home, aka
   Stay At Home

Tame

Vanilla

Verbena, aka Vervain

Violet

White Rose

Ylang Ylang

Luck Oils

Algiers Fast Luck	Lodestone
Anise	Lucky Month
Cinnamon	Lucky Planet
Devil's Shoestring	Magnet
Fast Luck	Red Fast Luck
Hindu	Road Opener
Jasmine	Tonka Bean

Legal Matters/Court Oils

Anise	Geranium
Bergamot	John the Conqueror
Crown of Success	Master
Domination	Special Favors
Galangal	Success

Money Oils

Bayberry	Lodestone
Chinese	Mandrake
Drawing	Money Draw, aka
Easy Life	Money Drawing
Jasmine	Showers of Gold
Jockey Club	Van Van
King Solomon	Wealthy Way
Lady Luck	

Peace Oils

All Spice
Benzoin
Crucible of Courage
French Lilac, aka Lilac
Geranium
Holy

Lavender
Lily
Orange
Sandalwood
Rose Geranium
White Rose

Planetary Oils

Sun
Moon
Venus
Mars

Mercury
Jupiter
Saturn

Power and Controlling Oils

American Voodoo
Baum de Commandeur
Bend Over
Boss Fix
Buddha
Calamus
Commanding
Compelling
Conquering
Devil's Shoestring
Domination

Essence of Bend Over,
   same as Bend Over
Fiery Command
Flaming Power
High John the Conqueror
King Solomon
Controlling
Master
Power
Seven Powers

Protection Oils

Bergamot
Counteracting
Five-finger Grass
Guinea
Jasper
Keep Away Enemies
Keep Away Hate
Keep Away Trouble
Lemon or Lemon Grass
Mandrake

Mecca
Nine Mystery
Oriental
Protection
Rose Geranium
Rose of Crucifixion
Sandalwood
Van Van
Fiery Wall of Protection
Wintergreen

Seduction Oils

Cinnamon (for women)
Clove (for men)
Civit
Fire of Love
Flame of Desire

Irresistible
Lyang Lyang
Vanilla
Verbena
Ylang Ylang

Success Oils

All Saints
Anointing
Balsam (same as
   Balsam of Peru)
Bible
Cassia
Cinnamon and
   Benzoin mixed
Consecration
Crown of Success

Crucible of Courage
Frankincense
Galbanum
Olibanum, same
   as Frankincense
Road Opener
Sesame
Spearmint
Success

Uncrossing, Hex Breaking, and Exorcism Oils

Counteracting
Dragon Blood
Evil Eye
Geranium
Jasper
Jinx Removing
Ju Ju
Myrrh
Nutmeg

Pine
Rose Geranium
Rue
Sassafras
Sesame
Uncrossing
Wall Breaker
Wormwood

Zodiacs

Aries
Taurus
Gemini
Cancer
Leo
Virgo
Libra

Scorpio
Sagittarius
Capricorn
Aquarius
Pisces
Zodiac

CHAPTER 6

THE PSALMS OF THE BIBLE

T he Psalms have long been used in supplication with candle burning and the prayers from the heart. Though the words of a Psalm may have no relationship with the problem with which it is associated, kabbalistically their recitation has proven to bring about change in the condition. As a quick reference, the Psalms are listed according to the particular situation.

For Illness or Pain

Psalm	Petition
2	For severe headaches.
3	When plagued with frequent headaches or backaches.
6	For healing of various diseases or pain in the eyes.
9	To restore the health of a male child.

Psalm	Petition
12	To protect from an injury or danger.
13	For serious eye problems.
15	For those with mental illness or depression.
18	When a sick person is having difficulty recovering.
20	Protection from pain or danger for twenty-four hours.
37	For safety while under an alcoholic influence.
49	To aid a person with a difficult fever.
67	To remove fever brought on by negative influences.
84	To remove body odors from a long illness.
89	For quick recovery from a long wasting illness.
91	For those troubled with an incurable disease.
102	To cure a three-day type of fever.
106	For fevers lasting three days.
107	For fevers lasting one day.
119:121–128	For pain in left hand or arm.
119:1–8	For those with palsy whose limbs quiver.
119:81–88	For swelling or infection on the right side of the nose.
119:57–64	To relieve pain in the torso.
119:25–32	To cure or remove pain from an injury to the left eye.
119:17–24	To restore the eyesight of an injured person.
119:145–152	To heal an injury to the left leg.
119:97–104	For pain or paralysis to the right hand or arm..

Psalm	Petition
119:129–136	For swelling or infection on the left side of the nose.
119:153–160	For pain and infection from a boil in the right ear.
119:169–176	For boils or infection of the left ear.
119:161–168	To relieve severe headaches.
119:65–72	For disease of hip, kidneys, or liver.
119:49–56	For those who are depressed or spiteful.
137	To recover from poisonous bites and stings of snakes or scorpions.
142	For pain in the thigh area.
143	For pain in the arms.
144	For the proper mending of a broken arm.
146	For healing of deep wounds or surgery.

For Business Situations

Psalm	Petition
5	For a business that doesn't prosper in spite of hard work or due to an opposing competitor.
8	To secure the love of all and have a good relationship in business.
36	To protect from unjust defamation of character.
63	When dealing with an unfair business partner, to help resolve problems without any losses.
82	For an agent to transact business satisfactorily with other countries.
108	For success in all business dealings.
114	For success in your occupation or business.

Concerning Bad Habits

Psalm	Petition
56	To be free of excessive habits of passion and to rid oneself of temptation of the senses.
59	To bring about a change within yourself by overcoming sinful appetites and emotions.
69	To free yourself from harmful and evil habits.
86	To do much good and avoid evil (best when said with 87 and 88).
117	To be forgiven for failing to keep a promise because you carelessly forgot.
119:1–8	For a person who finds it difficult to keep a promise.
119:9–16	To obtain a good memory. To acquire an understanding heart. To increase the desire to learn. To increase the intelligence.
131	To be more tolerant and subdue scornful pride (say three times a day).
132	To perform your duties and obligations promptly and punctually.
137	To release deep-rooted hate, envy, or spite from the heart.

In Dealing With an Enemy or Hostile Person

Psalm	Petition
7	To overcome an enemy plotting in secret against you.
9	To protect against the power and evil of an enemy.

Psalm	Petition
16	To reconcile with an enemy.
28	To have an enemy reconcile with you.
43	To regain your job lost because of malicious damage to your character.
43, 44, 45	To protect and overcome an unknown or known enemy.
44	To be safe from a hostile person.
48	To overcome people who hate you out of envy. To strike fear in your enemies.
70	To overcome an enemy in a just manner.
100	To stop an enemy's harassment.
110	For an enemy to seek reconciliation and peace.

In Matters of Faith

Psalm	Petition
80	To save one from falling into disbelief or from making other mistakes.
81	To keep one from losing their faith or making an error in judgment.
95	For a person of faith to help a confused and unbelieving neighbor.
99	For greater spiritual power.
115	To overcome spiritual scoffers and heretics.
118	To protect you from religious scoffers who try to lead you from the spiritual path.
119:33–40	To avoid temptations or vices.
119:73–80	To receive God's grace and find favor with man.

Psalm	Petition
129	To carry out good works and live within moral laws.
150	For praise and thankfulness for all answers received and to be received.

For Favors Wanted

Psalm	Petition
5	To receive a favor from a person in higher authority.
15	To be received by someone with approval.
21	To be received and accepted by someone in higher power when you see them.
32	To receive God's grace, mercy, and love.
34	When visiting an important person, so you'll be received with approval and have a pleasant visit.
85	To promote community welfare and church activity.
92	When you wish to attain and achieve high honors.
119:72–80	To receive the favor of man and God's g-race.
119:113–120	If about to meet with a person in a high position (say thirteen times).

For Crossed Conditions

Psalm	Petition
7	When others persecute you or try to harm or render you unsuccessful.
11	To be safe from harassment or evil.

Psalm	Petition
12	For overcoming oppressed feelings or influences.
14	To be free of insults or a lack of confidence.
16	To change an unhappy situation to a happy one.
31	To be free from the harm and irritation that idle gossip can cause.
41	To get your job back. For losing your job because your character has been slandered. To expose an enemy.
52	To be free from false accusations.
74	To stop harassment from an enemy.
83	To avoid being captured during war or to have a safe return.
101	To have protection from harmful vibrations given off by an evil person.
109	To protect from an enemy, persisting in bothering you.

Concerning Dreams

Psalm	Petition
23	To receive instructions or information through a dream or vision.
42	To learn the cause of a situation and desire the answer.

Confronting Fear or Danger

Psalm	Petition
11	To overcome fear and be safe from harassment.
20	To be free from anxiety or danger.

Psalm	Petition
24	To escape from serious danger.
25	To be protected from danger or harm.
26	When threatened by danger by water or land.
33	For protection from famine.
58	For protection from vicious dogs or dogs with rabies.
76	For protection from dangers of water or fire.
91	For protection from all kinds of dangers in life.
104	To prevent harm from spirits, persons or animals.
126	To protect a child's life during early years.
130	For safety.
141	When heavily oppressed by fears that concern you.
144–145	If you're disturbed by spirits, ghosts or apparitions.
148	To get a fire under control.

Concerning Friends

Psalm	Petition
47	To be liked by all.
85	To be reconciled with a former friend or lover (say with 123).
111	To have many more friends.
133	To keep the love and friendship of others. To have more friends.
138	To have the friendship and love of others.

Concerning Legal Problems

Psalm	Petition
5	To have mercy and favor in court.
7	If you fear an unfavorable verdict in your case in court.
20	When appearing before the judge to receive a favorable verdict.
35	To win a lawsuit. When opposed by an unjust or revengeful person.
38	When you fear the courts will not give you a just hearing. When appearing in court for the preliminary hearing.
93	To win your case in spite of a mean or unjust person.
119:25–32	To get advice and counsel helping your purpose in a lawsuit.
119:89–95	To receive justice and a favorable hearing in a lawsuit.
119:113–120	To ask a favor of an authority.
119:137–144	To prevent the judge or authority from being swayed by false information or misrepresentation.
119:49–56	To get out of a bad situation because of false or poor information given deliberately.

Concerning Luck

Psalm	Petition
4	To have good luck (repeat 3 times).
27	To be accepted in another city while traveling.
47	To be respected and loved by all.

Psalm	Petition
57	To have luck in what you do.
61	For luck and blessings when moving to a new home.
65	For all that you do to be fortunate and advantageous.
72	To live contentedly, free of lack and poverty.
96–98	To have joy, happiness, and peace within the family.
108	So that your departures from the home will be blessed.

Concerning Marriage

Psalm	Petition
45–46	To have peace between husband and wife.
113	To resolve disloyalty of a mate.
139	To keep and increase love in a marriage.
140	To remove increasing hate between husband and wife.

Concerning Negative Influences

Psalm	Petition
10	To remove negativity you feel around you often.
19	To rid oneself of strong negative influences.
29	To cast out an evil influence from another.
40	To free self from an evil influence.
59	To protect from being influenced from evil.
66	To help another overcome a negative influence.

90	To avoid disturbance by ghosts or apparitions.
91	Prayed over another bothered by negative influences.
104	To curb the desire to do wrong.

Concerning Pregnancy

Psalm   Petition

1	To prevent premature delivery.
10	For problems with delivery in pregnancy.
33	To protect an infant's life at the time of birth.
102	For a woman who has difficulty becoming pregnant (say with 103).
127	To protect a newborn from negative or evil influences.
128	To have a safe pregnancy and delivery.

Concerning Prison

Psalm   Petition

26	For someone in prison to have an early release.
71	Free another from prison confinement (seven times daily).
89	For the release of another who has been arrested.

Concerning Repenting

Psalm   Petition

51	To ease a troubled conscience.
62	To understand and resolve bad behavior.
74	To find pardon for morally wrong acts.

Psalm	Petition
99	To become more reverent.
135	To surrender your life to serve God.
136	To recognize willful transgressions and confess them.

Concerning Respect

Psalm	Petition
47	To be respected and liked by all.
78	To be loved and respected by those in high positions.
119:41–48	For another to work with you willingly and agreeably.

Concerning Thieves

Psalm	Petition
16	To discover a thief.
18	To frighten a robber away with no harm to you.
50	To be safe from any planned robbery or danger.

Concerning Safety

Psalm	Petition
12	To be safe from harassment because of differences.
13	To obtain safety for 24 hours.
20	To be free from all harm and distress.
30	To have safety from all negative influences or happenings.

Psalm	Petition
60	For a military person to be safe from injury and have a safe return home.
76	Freedom from threatening floods or fire.
116	To be protected from unnatural or sudden death.

Concerning School or Studies

Psalm	Petition
19	To be able to study and learn easily.
119:9–16	To improve your memory. To increase the desire to learn. To broaden the intelligence.
134	For those entering college.

Concerning Travel

Psalm	Petition
2	For protection while traveling over water.
6	To find help with trouble while traveling.
17	To be free from harm while traveling.
21	Safety from danger at sea during an approaching storm.
22	To avoid misfortune inflicted by human or animal.
34	To finish your journey safely.
64	For safety from accidents while traveling at sea.
120	For safe travel through an area infested with poisonous snakes.
122	For safety while traveling alone at night.
124	To overcome fear of traveling.

When using the Psalms it is best to use those that best fit your particular situation within each category. Always pray from your heart about the situation you are in and which you want to see changed for the better. Praying the Psalm without praying on your problem changes nothing.

CHAPTER 7

RITUAL COMPONENTS AND ALTERNATIVES

piritual cleansing prepares the individual for ritual prayer work by helping to remove negativity. One way to accomplish this is by using of incense to accompany your prayers. Other effective methods include taking a spiritual bath, or sweeping the aura clean of negative energy. The following discussion focuses on several methods for enhancing your ritual to make it more successful.

INCENSE

Incense comes in many forms: stick, cone, loose which is burned on charcoal, and self-lighting or spiritual. The spiritual incenses, also called "punk" incense, can be purchased prepackaged in 2½-ounce or 15-ounce boxes. This is good to keep on hand. It is self-lighting, it comes in various colors such as red, pink, purple, tan, green, black, and yellow, and if you run out of charcoal you can still use your loose incense blend. The technique is to blend one part of loose incense mixture with two parts of the spiritual incense, scoop it up into a cone, and light it with a match. The adage in all ritual work concerning incense is that any incense is better than no incense at all.

Spiritual incense also goes by various names such as: High John the Conqueror, Come to Me, Uncrossing, Fast Luck, Money Drawing, Success, etc. The name indicates the type of ritual it is used in.

As a guide to the use and making of ritual incense, consult the following: *Charms, Spells & Formulas* by Ray T. Malbrough; *The Complete Book of Incense, Oils and Brews* by Scott Cunningham; *Wylundt's Book of Incense* by Steven R. Smith; and *Incense* by Leo Vinci (see bibliography for publication data).

Incense is used in spiritual work to help remove stubborn negative conditions that a spiritual bath will not remove, by lifting the person's spirit to a higher level of vibration, thus bringing the person's protective spirits closer to him or her.

It is also used to spiritually clean your candles of all negative vibrations prior to dressing them, by passing them through the smoke as you pray.

BATHS AND FLOOR WASHES

In many spiritual supply houses you will find bottles of different colored liquids. These, like the spiritual incenses, also come with various names: Come to Me, Adam and Eve, Uncrossing, Jinx Remover, Money Drawing, Protection From Harm, Protection From Envy. Used by themselves, the baths and washes do nothing. Other ingredients must be added for these colored liquids to be effective on a spiritual level.

The role of these baths is to remove negative energy from the person's aura, conditioning it for spiritual work. The colors, when added to a spiritual bath, help to heal, condition, stabilize, and strengthen a chakra point within the person's body. The "blue" condition bath is excellent for strengthening and stabilizing the aura. When a chakra point becomes blocked, imbalances occur that affect the emotional and mental state of the person. These imbalances can adversely affect any ritual work or spell. Spiritual cleansing is very important for successful ritual work or spell casting. Spiritual cleansing is also very important to spiritual growth and development. A spiritual bath will not remove some negative conditions. The bath must be used in conjunction with a fumigation of the body with incense. Some will refer to this practice as smoking the body. The Amerindian practice of smudging can be followed by a spiritual bath.

Some of the baths and floor washes are simply labeled as Chinese wash and come in various colors: purple, green, yellow, pink, red, blue. These should be used with a mixture of ½ cup of epsom salt, 1 cup of table or sea salt, ¼ cup of baking soda, and 1 cup of apple cider vinegar. This is good for keeping the "etheric" body clean. All spiritual baths should contain at least ¼ cup of Holy or Consecrated water.

For ritual purposes, a tea is made using herbs associated with the type of ritual or spell. If for money, use herbs associated with money. If for love or marriage, use a combination of herbs for love. It's no big mystery. A healing bath uses herbs associated with health and healing.

Spiritual cleansing will give you protection from mild forms of hexing such as the evil eye caused by jealous people, by lifting the vibration of your spiritual body to a higher level than the negative energy flows on itself.

There are two methods of using a spiritual bath. One method is to put all the ingredients into a five-gallon bucket. After you take your soap bath, rinse your body by pouring the spiritual bath over your head and body, and leave the water to air dry on your skin. You may towel dry your hair slightly to remove excess water so that your hair will dry faster, preventing you from getting a head cold. The other method, which is preferable, is to fill the bathtub half-full with tap water. All ingredients for the bath are put into the tub. When stepping into the tub you should immerse yourself completely, getting your head wet under the water at least three times. Keep pouring the water over your body as you soak in the tub for ten to twenty minutes. Let the water air dry on your skin. Again you may slightly towel dry your hair to remove excessive water. In both methods of taking a spiritual bath it is very important to pray from your heart for the condition you want to see changed in your life.

As part of a spiritual cleansing, a technique called "sweeping" or brushing the aura is sometimes used. The wings of large birds or a bundle of fresh herbs are used to sweep away the negative energy that is loosened during the ritual by shaking a rattle or drumming. The drumming or shaking of the rattle is accompanied by chanted prayers. This type of cleansing is best done by a diviner priest/ess, voudun priest/ess, santero, or Indian shaman. A person can do this for themself if they are taught the proper method of smudging. Each time the aura is brushed with the herbs or bird wing, the ground is tapped, sending the negative energy into the earth. If the negative energy is not sent to be absorbed into the earth, it will simply fly around in the air to attach itself onto someone else.

It is a practice in Hoodoo/Voodoo, Santeria, and in the tribal religions of Africa to use live animals in this form of spiritual cleansing. After the animal is used, it is ritually sacrificed. Once the animal is used in this way, it is not possible to cook the animal for food. If you eat its flesh, you will absorb into your own person the negative energy contained within the body of the animal. In this instance it is best to use only the wings and feet of the bird for spiritual cleansing, saving the meat to be used for food.

Animal Sacrifice

Those who have read the section on "Honoring the Ancestors" and a brief description of the offerings may have been startled by the words "a live rooster is sacrificed to them." Animal sacrifice is a touchy subject. The local SPCA and animal rights activists have consistently condemned the practice as cruel and barbaric. Even Witches are opposed to the use of animal sacrifice, regarding it as senseless killing. As a practice within a religion, however, it is protected by the Constitution of the United States. It embodies the expression of the religion's faith. The word "sacrifice" comes from Latin, meaning to make sacred: *Sacer* (sacred) and *facere* (to make).

Many people might be surprised to learn that the use of animal sacrifice was a part of medieval Ceremonial Magick practice. The system is referred to as High Magick by many esoteric orders such as the Golden Dawn, and others using the kabbala. David Conway, in his *Magic, An Occult Primer*, describes in his Latin version of the "Kabbalistic Master Ritual" how animal sacrifice was used in releasing power. He states that the animal was decapitated and the practice was messy, cruel, and unnecessary. Naturally, if you cut an animal's head off, blood will spurt out everywhere. Conway writes that the magician would either drink the blood or if the magician was squeamish, would plunge his or her hands into the blood at the same time the intention was willed in the normal manner. Then Conway said it was more common to use sex to attain the desired outcome. Is it better for the animal to die than yourself from catching an STD (Sexually Transmitted Disease) or HIV and AIDS?

The Key of Solomon the King (Clavicula Salomonis), page 119, Book II, Chapter XXII contains the section: "Concerning Sacrifices to the Spirits, and How They Should Be Made." The instructions specify that the animals be virgin quadrupeds or birds. In this case the bird is usually a dove. It is further stated that white animals are sacrificed to the good spirits and black animals to the evil spirits. These instructions are accompanied by the prayers used in making the sacrifice.

It has been my personal experience that no matter how opposed an individual may be to animal sacrifice, he or she will not hesitate for one moment to avail themselves of its power when all other approaches have failed. Blood is a very powerful fluid condenser, and in magico-religious practice animal sacrifice is done only if it is indicated through divination. It is not done, nor should it be, just for the sake of killing. This is not a practice that is taken lightly.

Though it is possible to perform acts of magick without the use of animal sacrifice or sex practices, it is hard work. Witches know this from firsthand experience. Their method of raising energy (power) to be released in order to perform a positive change may have to be done more than once to achieve any results. It all depends on the type of situation and the results they wish to achieve. A witch's form of sympathetic magick is similar to the magick practiced in voodoo. Their charm bags or magick pillows are similar to the wanga/mojo/gris-gris of voodoo. Their use of candles in spell casting is similar to the use of candles in voodoo. The magical use of stones and herbs in folk magick is nearly the same in both European and African practice. The witches' practice of dancing in a circle to raise power is also used by some African tribes, as well as in the Macumba rituals in Brazil and some voodoo dances in Haiti. Amuletic and Talismanic magick is practiced by both witches and ceremonial magicians as well as the Bokor in Haiti and the practitioners of Brazil, but ceremonial magicians insist on labeling sympathetic magick, folk spells, and candle magick as low magick. Magick is designed to get results in the mundane world, not to remain in the spiritual realm. It was once said to me by a magician, "Scorn the ladder on which you stand; it will fall out from under you."

CHAPTER 8

THE MYSTICAL NOVENA: PUTTING IT ALL TOGETHER

rt imitates life" is a saying often used; it could also be said that religion imitates magick. The Practice of Magick is far older than today's religions; in ancient times there were priest magicians in all cultures. In the first few hundred years of Christianity in Europe, many of the churches had double altars; the new god Christ was worshipped on one altar and the pagan deities worshipped on another. The early priests may have taken communion on Sunday, but come the full moon they may have also danced in the woods celebrating the Old Ways. It is a known fact that many of the cathedrals of Europe were built on the established sites of pagan worship. Even when Christianity was finally able to outlaw pagan practices, it still owed a debt to pagan inspiration and influence.

187

Keeping this in mind, it is not surprising to learn that a pagan practice continues today. One of the most powerful rituals in candle magick is also practiced by the followers of the Roman Catholic church. This type of devotion is referred to simply as a "novena." A novena is a special prayer enacted for nine consecutive days. Even though the novena is associated with Christianity today, its origins spring from the magickal rites of pagan times The number nine has long been connected with the moon.

Concentrated effort is the key to success in any magickal ritual that requires dedication, discipline, and hark work. This is what is required when performing the mystical novena. A constant repetition of a ritual directed to an end result will stir the Powers into action.

This is the way it all works:

Any magick worked through the novena operates on the same principle as the brick under the dripping faucet we talked about earlier. The energy generated by your prayer, combined with the burning of candles over a period of time, will dissolve any and all obstacles in the way of success.

Generally Catholics only invoke the assistance of a saint who has become associated with the particular problem the person may face in their current situation, but many occultists, witches, or magicians may also bring in another element, making a mystical novena by invoking either the Planetary Angels or the pagan deities of his or her pantheon of choice. These can be Celtic, Norse, Egyptian, Hindu, Greek, or Roman—it matters not—because the angelic beings and pagan deities are symbolic images of cosmic forces which are clothed in archetypal forms. Many of the Catholic saints were pagan deities in disguise taken over by the early church when paganism was prohibited. Since the populace refused to abandon their worship, the church simply canonized them as saints.

During the actual novena, all the candles used must be kept burning all the time if possible. The ritual should be performed for a nine-day period. In today's fast-paced society this can be impractical. However, the novena can be worked over a twenty-four-hour period, and there are those who work their novena nine hours a day, for nine days. The point is that the candles must be kept burning all the time as you are working the mystical novena.

Some people may use seven different lights to represent the Planetary Angels; however, one seven-day vigil light in seven different colors is sufficient. In the mystical novena, your prayer is sent out each hour for nine hours, for nine days. This is why you must tend to the candles at all times; none should be allowed to go out during the novena. The candles representing your prayer and their burning are setting up a pressure to first remove the obstacles in the way, then a pressure to bring about the desired outcome of your prayer—manifesting itself in reality.

A contemporary method of working with the Planetary angels is as follows, beginning with midnight:

Hour	Angel	Pagan Deity
00:00–01:00	Sachiel	the Dagda, Jupiter, Thor, Zeus
01:00–02:00	Anael	Epona, Aphrodite, Eros, Freya, Isis
02:00–03:00	Uriel	Cernunnos, Arianrhod, Nerthus, Gaea
03:00–04:00	Cassiel	Anubis, Bran, Cronos, the Norns
04:00–05:00	Micheal	Apollo, Brighid, Helios, Ra, Lugh
05:00–06:00	Gabriel	Artemis, Diana, Hathor, Hecate, Selene
06:00–07:00	Samael	Aries, Mars, Tiw, the Morrigu
07:00–08:00	Raphael	Athene, Hermes, Mercury, Woden, Ogma
08:00–09:00	Sachiel	the Dagda, Jupiter, Thor, Zeus
09:00–10:00	Anael	Epona, Aphrodite, Eros, Freya, Isis
10:00–11:00	Uriel	Cernunnos, Arianrhod, Nerthus, Gaea
11:00–12:00	Cassiel	Anubis, Bran, Cronos, the Norns
12:00–01:00	Micheal	Apollo, Brighid, Helios, Ra, Lugh
01:00–02:00	Gabriel	Artemis, Diana, Hathor, Hecate, Selene
02:00–03:00	Samael	Aries, Mars, Tiw, the Morrigu
03:00–04:00	Raphael	Athene, Hermes, Mercury, Woden, Ogma
04:00–05:00	Sachiel	the Dagda, Jupiter, Thor, Zeus
05:00–06:00	Anael	Epona, Aphrodite, Eros, Freya, Isis
06:00–07:00	Uriel	Cernunnos, Arianrhod, Nerthus, Gaea
07:00–08:00	Cassiel	Anubis, Bran, Cronos, The Norns
08:00–09:00	Micheal	Apollo, Brigh, Helios, Ra, Lugh
09:00–10:00	Gabriel	Artemis, Diana, Hathor, Hecate, Selene
10:00–11:00	Samael	Aries, Mars, Tiw, the Morrigu
11:00–12:00	Raphael	Athene, Hermes, Mercury, Woden, Ogma

Three of the angels in the list of hours are also saints in the Catholic tradition: Michael, Raphael, and Gabriel. Today many witches do invoke the protective powers of these three angels, as well as the angel Uriel, when constructing sacred space in their rituals, a proof that the angels come to the aid and assistance of Christians and non-Christians alike. If witches were truly evil, as Fundamental Christian leaders want the public to believe, then these angels would not help the witches as they have been doing and will continue to do. Enough said. For greater detail in study on angels I would recommend you read *Angels: Companions In Magick* by Silver RavenWolf (Llewellyn Publications, 1995).

The pagan deities listed with the hours are simply intended to give some inspiration to those who walk the pagan path to spirituality. This bit of information may help them to learn better to associate their chosen pantheon with the planetary hours instead of using the planetary angels.

To begin the mystical novena you will need to look in the following correspondences associated with the Planetary angel to determine the angel's sphere of influence in human life. These are as follows:

Michael's influence concerns creating peace and harmony, obtaining the favor of those in high places (this can mean your boss or immediate supervisor at work), riches, honor, glory, making friends, physical health, ambition, career, success, personal finances, sports.

Gabriel's influence concerns reconciliations, dreams, receptivity, love, voyages (to encourage good or safe travel), female fertility, the home, psychic powers, women.

Samael is concerned with influencing activities associated with developing courage, overthrowing enemies, military honors, breaking negative conditions, protection from fire and violence, sexual energy, men, manual dexterity.

Raphael gives assistance in matters concerning health, science, studies, psychic and spiritual development, communications, divination, influencing others, memory, commerce, writing, acting, education, travel, finding lost objects or stolen property.

Sachiel influences matters of wealth, obtaining luck, male fertility, friendship, health, social status, political power, big business, gambling, legal and insurance matters.

Anael rules over situations involving love, romance, beauty, kindness, happiness, travel, to foster new friendships, to gratify lust, marital affairs, the environment, music, fashion, and the arts.

Uriel influences such matters as harmony, balance, legal counsel, relationships, lawyers, income, strength, planning, assets.

Cassiel rules over matters concerning old people, karma, psychic self-defense, spirit communication to protect from evil, inheritances, property, death, agriculture.

Once the angel is determined, you would begin the mystical novena within the angel's assigned hour; for example you want to begin a novena to sell your home or business. In the list of saints we see that St. Philomena is associated with real estate and we would begin the novena in the hour assigned to the angel Cassiel, for this angel influences matters connected with property. The hour of Cassiel is 11:00 A.M. through noon. To perform the novena you must continue each hour with the appropriate prayer, for nine consecutive hours, invoking the saint and each of the angels in turn.

1st hour   St. Philomena and Cassiel.

2nd hour   St. Philomena, Cassiel, and Michael.

3rd hour   St. Philomena, Cassiel, Michael, and Gabriel.

4th hour   St. Philomena, Cassiel, Michael, Gabriel, and Samael.

5th hour   St. Philomena, Cassiel, Michael, Gabriel, Samael, and Raphael.

6th hour   St. Philomena, Cassiel, Michael, Gabriel, Samael, Raphael and Sachiel.

7th hour   St. Philomena, Cassiel, Michael, Gabriel, Samael, Raphael, Sachiel, and Anael.

8th hour   St. Philomena, Cassiel, Michael, Gabriel, Samael, Raphael, Sachiel, Anael, and Uriel.

9th hour   St. Philomena, Cassiel, Michael, Gabriel, Samael, Raphael, Sachiel, Anael, Uriel, and finally Cassiel again.

This sequence is repeated daily for nine days, always beginning in the hour of the angel associated with your problem. When you are working your novena in this way you are invoking not only one of the planetary Angels but the whole combined power force of the Angelic Hierarchy.

In the above example, to sell your home or business, you would also use the candle setup to Attract Success (number 33), with a candle in honor of St. Philomena and a seven-colored candle to represent the Angelic Hierarchy. Given a little thought and imagination, any situation that occurs in life can be handled by taking time to consult the associations between the saints and the angelic hierarchy. Combine this with the candle setups given in this book, and you will find the necessary help to solve your problems in life. It is said, "It is better to light a candle than to curse the darkness."

THE PRAYERBINDER CHAPLET

Rosaries, chaplets, prayer beads—whatever they are called—beads have been used for centuries as an instrument of religious devotion in Roman Catholicism and in Buddhism. Prayer beads can be wonderful tools in measuring out the time spent in prayer; devotions for each bead are represented by your recited prayers.

The standard Roman Catholic rosary, when done correctly, will aid the individual in learning to use creative visualization in conjunction with vocal prayer. In practice, when the rosary is recited the person is supposed to visualize themselves present as the mystery is unfolding or meditate on a fixed image of the mystery as they say each decade of ten Hail Marys. To recite the standard rosary without mental visualization is considered fruitless.

Chaplets are similar to the Buddhist rosaries, and are used when invoking the assistance of a particular saint during your novena. There are chaplets of St. Anthony, St. Ann, St. Joseph, the Infant Jesus of Prague, the Sacred Heart of Jesus, and a chaplet of St. Jude. Naturally these chaplets include prayers to the saint to whom they are directed.

The Prayerbinder Chaplet is inspired from the chaplet of St. Anthony. In using the chaplet of St. Anthony you recite for each bead an Our Father, a Hail Mary, and a Gloria, thirteen times. The number thirteen is associated with St. Anthony. There are thirteen full moons in a year.

Within the nine metaphysical or occult laws, the Law of Three Requests states that all requests from the subtle dimensions are to be repeated in triplicate. The first utterance alerts the conscious mind, the second repetition engages the reasoning faculties, while the third repetition of the prayer makes direct contact with the psyche or soul force. For this reason all prayers or petitions are recited three times.

It has also been said about prayer that a prayer said seven times will be believed by all who hear it. However, a prayer that is said nine times will be answered by God. In this case each triplet (group of three beads) is repeated nine times. Three times nine equals twenty-seven and two plus seven equals nine. Nine is the number of the moon. The triplet can represent the goddess as Maiden, Mother, Crone.

In use, the first nine Triplets are ended with a positive affirmation borrowed from a traditional form of magick used by Witches. The last four Triplets invoke the elements of Fire, Water, Earth, and Air, again part of a traditional spell in Witchcraft. I will not give these two spells in this book but a knowledgeable witch will recognize the two spells by the words alone. See the Chaplet illustration (opposite). The affirmations and invocations of the elements are as follows:

> *By Triplet of one, my prayer is begun.*
> *By Triplet of two, my prayer cometh true.*
> *By Triplet of three, thus my prayer shall now be.*
> *By Triplet of four, opens the door.*
> *By Triplets of five my prayer is alive.*
> *By Triplet of six, my prayer I now fix.*
> *By Triplet of seven, events I now leaven.*
> *By Triplet of eight, my prayer is now fate.*
> *By Triplet of nine, this prayer is mine.*

At Earth, say:
> *I call earth to bind my prayer spell.*

At Air, say:
> *Air to speed its travel well.*

At Fire, say:
> *Fire to give it spirit from above.*

At Water, say:
> *Water bless my prayer with love. So be it!*

The prayerbinder chaplet is composed of thirty-nine beads. The number thirty-nine can be broken down to a single digit, the number three. Three plus nine equals twelve, and one plus two equals three. Your actual prayer is recited on each of the thirty-nine beads, ending the Triplet with the appropriate affirmation.

Prayerbinder Chaplet inspired from the Chaplet of
St. Anthony. For a Pagan, the St. Anthony medal can be
replaced by a Pentacle.

YOUR PRAYER FROM THE HEART

Try to make your prayer from the heart a positive statement happening now, but in rhyme. This technique in using the chaplet can be applied to any of life's situations and will give you fifteen to twenty minutes of focused concentration on your desire, while using the chaplet as part of your novena.

Prayer and candle burning have long been an established practice among Roman Catholics, the largest Christian denomination in North and South America.

Never, ever, pray "If it be your will, Lord." You will be setting yourself up for your prayer to not be answered.

CHAPTER 9

ON BECOMING A DIVINER PRIEST OR PRIESTESS

ost cultures where magick is an accepted part of daily life require different levels of the priesthood within their society. This is true of most Nature-based religions, for there are priests and priestesses whose main function is to oversee that the religious rituals of its culture are carried out correctly. These people must know the culture's mythology, songs, and prayers as well as the order in which the rituals are to be performed. Then there are those who are trained in the art of divination. Before any ritual is performed, divination is done to assure that the religious ceremony will be pleasing to the deities and to determine what type of offerings the deities may be requesting at the time of the celebration.

In Nigeria and in the Santeria cult in the New World, diviner priests are exclusively male (women are excluded from this type of priesthood). These initiated men are called "baba-lawos," and are considered the High Priests of the religion.

In Louisiana this is not the case; the diviner may be either male or female. We know from the ancient Greeks that the Pythoness was the title of the priestess who delivered the answers of Apollo to those who came to consult the oracle at Delphi. True psychic ability does not know gender, but will manifest itself easily in any male or female whose destiny it is to be a diviner. Therefore, the technique is only taught to those individuals who the oracle itself says are to be initiated into the diviner priesthood. It makes no difference how psychic a person may think they are, the deities themselves choose through the geomantic patterns who they want to fulfill the function of diviner priest or priestess within the society. This has provided members of the community with a safeguard from being duped of their hard-earned money.

There is in actual practice one exception to the rule of the oracle being taught to those who are chosen through the oracle itself. That exception is that it is possible to keep the practice within one's family lineage, from generation to generation. The ancestors may choose to speak through the patterns, for the ancestors are invoked by prayer at the commencement of the divination session.

The initiation ceremony to become a diviner lasts thirty-three days. This can be difficult for those who are married, since during the initiation period the individual must be kept separate from friends and especially from their family.

Abstinence from any form of sexual activity is required during this initiatory period.

After completing the study of the sortilege technique, one would have been required to memorize the sixteen basic meanings to the geomantic patterns, the five basic patterns that answer questions, the fifteen combinations borne from the five patterns, 135 commentaries to the double geomantic patterns that are formed within the system, plus the commentary made by the sixteen basic patterns doubled. This is a total of 151 different commentaries.

The system commonly used in European geomancy, illustrated in the teachings of the *Golden Dawn, Three Books of Occult Philosophy*, and of interest in *A Witch's Book of Divination* by Callia Underhill (all published by Llewellyn Publications, 1989, 1993. and 1996) is worthy of study. This system makes use of three geomantic patterns, arriving at a final interpretation in with only 128 meanings. I have not personally seen this system used in magico-religious practice, but it is of interest.

The system that I was taught originally is rooted in the principles of living in harmony with Nature. This is done by placing all the elements of the self (head, heart, spirit, and soul) in alignment with the individual's personal destiny. Once the elements of the self are placed in alignment with the individual's personal destiny, the person is placed in alignment with spiritual evolution.

Nature is essentially benevolent. Therefore, to be in harmony with Nature is rooted in the ethic of building strong, moral character. This results in the balancing of the polar forces which influence the interaction between the self and the world. As a result, those who develop strong, moral character can experience health, abundance, and wisdom. This does not mean that problems will disappear; they won't. But being in balance with the self and the world will generate the wisdom to solve problems effectively. By being in harmony with Nature the wisdom is constantly being nurtured and developed. It is the task of the diviner Priest or Priestess to identify the forces which are pulling the client away from experiencing true inner peace and harmony. This forms the basis for identifying the source of imbalance between the self and the World. The process of restoring balance is known as changing bad fortune to good fortune.

THE GEOMANTIC PATTERNS

The basic geomantic patterns are as follows:

1. I   *Latin name:* Via
    I   *African name:* Ogbe
    I   *Gender:* Male
    I   *Element:* Water
         Associated planet: Moon
         Zodiac sign: Cancer

Deities speaking in this pattern are according to the Louisiana Voodoo pantheon: Marassa le flambeau, Madame la lune (Mrs. Moon), and Marassa. The Catholic saint associated here is St. Joseph.

2.   I I   *Latin name:* Populus
     I I   *African name:* Oyeku
     I I̊   *Gender:* Female
     I I   *Element:* Water
           Associated planet: Moon
           Zodiac sign: Cancer

In this pattern the Voudan pantheon of Via speaks, as well as the dead known as the Guedeh and the ancestors. St. Peter is the associated Catholic saint in this geomantic pattern.

3.   I I   *Latin name:* Conjunctio
     I   *African name:* Iwori
     I   *Gender:* Male
     I I   *Element:* Earth
           Associated planet: Mercury
           Zodiac sign: Virgo

Within the contemporary Voodoo pantheon of Louisiana, the following speak through this pattern: Simbi, Simbi la flambeau, Simbi de'leau, Ossange. Catholic saint: St. Christopher.

4.   I   *Latin name:* Carcer
     I I   *African name:* Odi or Idi
     I I   *Gender:* Female
     I   *Element:* Earth
           Associated planet: Saturn
           Zodiac sign: Capricorn

Here speaking according to the Voodoo pantheon of Louisiana are: the Guedeh, Maman Brigitte, Marassa, Guedeh la flambeau. The Catholic saints associated here are St. Rita and St. Augustine.

5.   I   *Latin name:* Fortuna Minor
      I   *African name:* Irosun
      I I   *Gender:* Female, African gender: Male
      I I   *Element:* Fire
             Associated planet: Sun
             Zodiac sign: Leo

Within the Louisiana Voodoo pantheon speaking in this geomantic pattern are: Legba la flambeau, Dan-i, Legba. Saint
Theresa, the Little Flower, is the Catholic saint associated here.

6.   I I   *Latin name:* Fortuna Major
      I I   *African name:* Owonrin
      I   *Gender:* Male, African gender: Female
      I   *Element:* Fire
             Associated planet: Sun
             Zodiac sign: Leo

Within this pattern the Guedeh from the Voodoo pantheon of
Louisiana speak, as well as Legba, Dan-i, Legba la flambeau.
The Catholic saints are: St. Benedict, St. Expedite, St. Anthony.

7.   I   *Latin name:* Laetitia
      I I   *African name:* Obara
      I I   *Gender:* Female, African gender: male
      I I   *Element:* Water
             Associated planet: Jupiter
             Zodiac sign: Pisces

Of the Louisiana Voodoo pantheon speak: Agwe la flambeau,
La Baleine (Bhalin'dio), Agwe. The Catholic saints are St. Francis of Assisi, and the Infant Jesus of Prague.

8. I I *Latin name:* Tristitia
    I I *African name:* Okanra
    I I *Gender:* male, African gender: female
    I   *Element:* Air
         Associated planet: Saturn
         Zodiac sign: Aquarius

According to the Louisiana Voodoo panthenon speak: the Guedah, Maman Brigitte, Guedeh la flambeau, Marassa. St. Anthony, St. Expedite, St. Theresa, and Saints. Cosmus and Damien are the Catholic saints.

9. I   *Latin name:* Cauda Draconis
    I   *African name:* Ogunda
    I   *Gender:* Male
    I I *Element:* Fire
         Associated planet: None. It is related to the moon's south node. However there are some who assign this pattern to both Saturn and Mars.
         Zodiac sign: Scorpio

Within the Louisiana Voodoo pantheon speak: Ogou la flambeau, Ogou Bhalin'dio, Ogou ferraille, Ogou Badagris, the Guedeh, and Baron Samedi. The Catholic saints ascribed to this pattern are: St. John the Baptist, St. James the Elder, St. Joseph, St. George, and St. Joan of Arc.

10. I I   *Latin name:* Caput Draconis

    I   *African name:* Osa

    I   *Gender:* Female

    I   *Element:* Earth

        Associated planet: None. It is related to the moon's north node. However, there are some who assign this pattern to both Jupiter and Venus.

Speaking from the Louisiana Voodoo pantheon are: Damballah, Aido We'do, Aizan, Damballah la flambeau. The Catholic saints are: St. Patrick, and the Blessed Mother Ascending to Heaven.

11. I I   *Latin name:* Rubeus or Rubeo

    I   *African name:* Ika

  I I   *Gender:* Male

  I I   *Element:* Water

        Associated planet: Mars

        Zodiac sign: Scorpio

In the pantheon of Louisiana Voodoo speaking here are all aspects of Ogou. The Catholic saints are: St. John the Baptist, St. James the Elder, St. Joseph, St. George, St. Joan of Arc, the Guardian Angel, St. Matthew, St. Mark, St. Luke, and St. John.

12. I I   *Latin name:* Albeo or Albeus

  I I   *African name:* Oturupon

    I   *Gender:* Female

  I I   *Element:* Air

        Associated planet: Mercury

        Zodiac sign: Gemini

The associated pantheon within Louisiana Voodoo are: Legba and all aspects of Simbi. The Catholic saints are: St. Anthony, the Holy Trinity, St. Raphael Archangel.

13.   I   *Latin name:* Puella
      I I   *African name:* Otura
      I   *Gender:* Female, African gender: Male
      I   *Element:* Air
             Associated planet: Venus
             Zodiac sign: Libra

Within the pantheon of Louisiana Voodoo today speak La Sirene, Erzulie, Erzulie Dantor, Erzulie la flambeau, Erzulie Freda Dahomey. Catholic saints are Our Lady of Grace, the Sacred Heart of Jesus, St. Martha.

14.   I   *Latin name:* Puer
      I   *African name:* Irete
      I I   *Gender:* Male, African gender: Female
      I   *Element:* Fire
             Associated planet: Mars
             Zodiac sign: Aries

Speaking from the Louisiana Voodoo pantheon are: Ogou la flambeau, Ogou Bhalin'dio, Ogou Ferraille. The Catholic saints are: St. James the Elder, St. Joseph, St. Anthony, St. Peter, St. George, St. Joan of Arc, a litany to all the saints.

15. I   *Latin name:* Amissio
     I I   *African name:* Ose
     I   *Gender:* Female, African gender: Male
     I I   *Element:* Earth
           Associated planet: Venus
           Zodiac sign: Taurus

All aspects of Erzulie as well as La Sirene speak from the
Louisiana Voodoo today. The associated Catholic saints are St.
Cecilia and St. Philomena.

16. I I   *Latin name:* Aqusito
     I   *African name:* Ofun
     I I   *Gender:* Male, African gender: Female
     I   *Element:* Fire
           Associated planet: Jupiter
           Zodiac sign: Sagittarius

Within the contemporary Louisiana pantheon of Voodoo
speak: La Baleine (Bhalin'dio), Agwe, Agwe la flambeau. The
Catholic saints are: St. Expedite and Our Lady, Star of the Sea.

Within each of the above sixteen geomagnetic patterns there
are three levels of interpretation: a basic meaning, a cautionary
meaning, and a proverb. Both the cautionary meaning and the
proverb deal with the spiritual issues involved with the question, as well as give wisdom and advice. The commentary that
the double geomantic patterns make tells something about the
client to the diviner. For instance: is the client telling the truth
to the diviner or not, is the client a hypochondriac or having a

substance abuse problem, functioning sexually, or is the client perhaps being dominated by a partner, etc.?

No diviner priest or priestess makes any claims to know all or see all, because there is no future guaranteed in the western sense of the word "future." Inconstancy is the only guarantee in life. Basically there is only the past, which is the foundation on which we all stand. Then there is only the present. The present is something that constantly changes, evolves, and comes into being. Much of what we will experience will be in harmony with the thoughts that are constantly kept in our minds and regularly nourished by our emotions. Both the conscious mind or thoughts and the emotions influence the subconscious mind, which only takes orders. Much of the negative experiences a person may undergo on a consistent basis are a direct result of negative programming within their subconscious mind. To automatically believe that every time you have bad luck in any area of your life someone has put a curse on you is superstition. When you learn to change any and all negative thinking, you can change your life for the better. It bears repeating: any card reader, psychic, Hoodoo practitioner, root worker, etc. who attempts to instill fear and superstition in a client's mind is no good and it would be best to have nothing to do with them in the future.

Three things that can never be changed in a person's life: the day you were born, the day you will die, and another person's character. Everything else in life is subject to change for good or bad.

CHAPTER 10

ALL SAINTS CHAPEL
OF FAITH

ll Saints Chapel of Faith is a non-denominational church. As a non-profit organization, its ordained ministers are trained in the use and function of magico-religious divination as a tool used in counseling, helping others to solve their problems.

All ministers must undergo a strict, disciplined period of spiritual training, using various spiritual exercises designed to aid the growth and development of psychic and spiritual potential.

During their training prior to ordination, all ministers study comparative religion and the background of the thirty-three major religious traditions.

In keeping to the United States Constitution's Amendment for the freedom of religion, the ministers of All Saints Chapel of Faith have the freedom to express their personal ministry in the spiritual paths of Spiritualism/Spiritism, Wicca/Neo-Pagan, and Louisiana Voodoo/Hoodoo. Once the spiritual path is chosen, the minister in training is also given detailed instruction in the religion selected.

All ordained ministers can legally perform marriages after registering in the Parish (County) Seat in which they reside.

Many Parishes (counties) have ordinances against the practice of any type of fortunetelling within their jurisdiction, except by an ordained minister of a valid, registered church functioning in the State of Louisiana.

The documents that are reproduced here have been included in this chapter as validation of All Saints Chapel of Faith.

The Author's Certificate of Ordination as a Minister.

UNITED STATES OF AMERICA
State of Louisiana

Fox McKeithen
SECRETARY OF STATE

As Secretary of State, of the State of Louisiana, I do hereby Certify that

a copy of the Articles of Incorporation of

ALL SAINTS CHAPEL OF FAITH

Domiciled at New Orleans, Louisiana, Parish of Orleans,

A corporation organized under the provisions of R.S. 1950, Title 12, Chapter 2, as amended,

By Act before a Notary Public in and for the Parish of Orleans, State of Louisiana, on June 2, 1993, the date when corporate existence began,

Was filed and recorded in this Office on June 3, 1993, in the Record of Non-Profit Corporations Book 344,

And all fees having been paid as required by law, the corporation is authorized to transact business in this State, subject to the restrictions imposed by law, including the provisions of R. S. 1950, Title 12, Chapter 2, as amended.

In testimony whereof, I have hereunto set my hand and caused the Seal of my Office to be affixed at the City of Baton Rouge on,

June 3, 1993

KGU   *Secretary of State*

Articles of Incorporation of All Saints Chapel of Faith, the State of Louisiana.

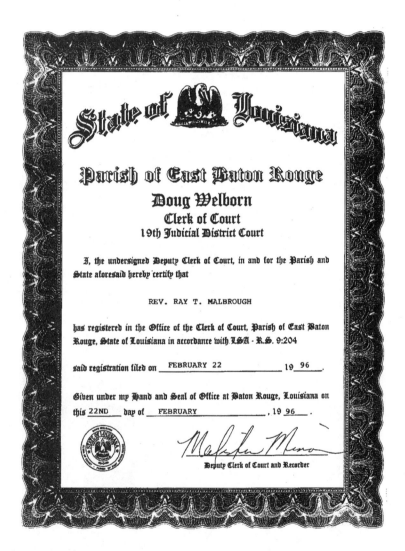

State of Louisiana

Parish of East Baton Rouge

Doug Welborn
Clerk of Court
19th Judicial District Court

I, the undersigned Deputy Clerk of Court, in and for the Parish and State aforesaid hereby certify that

REV. RAY T. MALBROUGH

has registered in the Office of the Clerk of Court, Parish of East Baton Rouge, State of Louisiana in accordance with LSA - R.S. 9:204

said registration filed on ___FEBRUARY 22___ 19_96_.

Given under my Hand and Seal of Office at Baton Rouge, Louisiana on this _22ND_ day of ___FEBRUARY___, 19_96_.

Deputy Clerk of Court and Recorder

The Author's Registration Document as a minister in the Parish of East Baton Rouge, Louisiana.

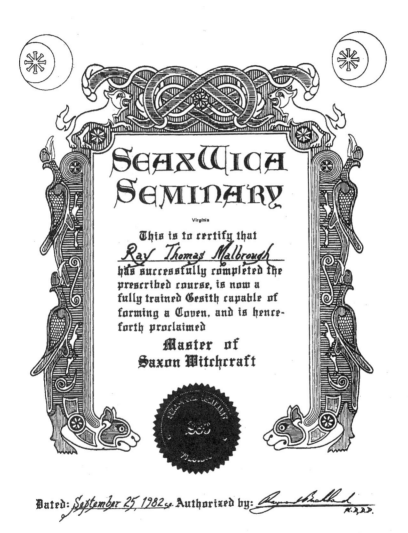

SeaxWica Seminary

Virginia

This is to certify that

Ray Thomas Malbrough

has successfully completed the prescribed course, is now a fully trained Gesith capable of forming a Coven, and is henceforth proclaimed

Master of Saxon Witchcraft

Dated: *September 25, 1982*. Authorized by: _____

R.D.D.

Document attesting to the author's completion of training in the
Seax Wica Seminary, Virginia, signed by Raymond Buckland.

CHAPTER XI

A FINAL WORD OF ADVICE

hen seeking out a person for assistance with your personal problems, it does not matter what they may call themselves: witch, voodoo priest/ess, hoodoo worker, santero, santera, palero, palera, spiritualist, mother this, sister that, reverend so-and-so; listen to me well. If that person begins to instill fear and superstition in your mind, they are no good. Run in the opposite direction—have nothing to do with them. Their only aim is to set you up in order to exploit you for every bit of your money that they can get their hands on. Don't become a victim out of fear that they will put some sort of evil spell on you because you do not want to be their client. It is your civil right to choose whom you want to patronize.

One practitioner in the New Orleans area once told me that, "fear is better than love." Well, I know that this person is a thief, ripping off his clients, selling them spiritual baths that contain nothing but one ounce of perfume to a gallon of water. His clients are paying the going rate of $25.00 for a gallon bath. Men and women who are superstitious and the love-torn are prime targets of exploitation.

When it comes to choosing a spiritual practitioner, take your time and select one whom you trust. Trust cannot be of a blind type. Trust is something that is earned, not given away. Spiritual practitioners should strive to earn your trust, before you trust them with your life and money. Feel them out first by getting a reading from time to time, but do not be so eager to pay them money to do spiritual work for you. They may take your money but there is no guarantee they will do the work.

Bibliography

Buckland, Raymond. *Practical Candleburning Rituals*. St. Paul: Llewellyn Publications, 1970.

—————. *Advanced Candle Magick*. St. Paul: Llewellyn Publications, 1996.

—————. *Secrets of Gypsy Fortune Telling*. St. Paul: Llewellyn Publications, 1988.

—————. *The Tree: Complete Book of Saxon Witchcraft* . York Beach, ME: Samuel Weiser, 1995)

Cunningham, Scott. *Cunningham's Encyclopedia of Magical Herbs*. St. Paul: Llewellyn Publications, 1985.

—————. *The Complete Book of Incense, Oils & Brews*. St. Paul: Llewellyn Publications, 1994.

Buckland, Raymond, and Kathleen Binger. *The Book of African Divination*. U.S. Games, 1997.

Chisholm, James Allen. *True Hearth*. Runa-Raven Press, 1993.

Fatunmbi, Awo Fa Lokun. *Awo Ifa and the Theology of Orisha Divination*. Bronx, New York: Original Publications, 1992.

Howard, Michael. *Finding Your Guardian Angel.* New York: Thorsons: Harper Collins Publishers, 1996.

Mickaharic Draja. *Practice of Magic.* York Beach, ME: Samuel Weiser, Inc. 1995

Neimark, John Philip. *The Way of the Orisa.* New York: Harper Collins Publishers, 1993.

Pajeon, Kala and Ketz. *The Candle Magick Workbook.* Secaucus, NJ: Carol Publishing Group,1991.

Regardie, Israel. *Golden Dawn.* St. Paul: Llewellyn Publications, 1989

Sherwood, Keith. *The Art of Spiritual Healing.* St. Paul: Llewellyn Publications, 1995.

Silver RavenWolf. *Angels: Companions in Magick.* St. Paul: Llewellyn Publications, 1996.

_____. *Hex Craft: Dutch Country Pow-Pow Magick.* St. Paul: Llewellyn Publications, 1995.

Silver RavenWolf & Nigel Jackson. *The Rune Oracle.* St. Paul: Llewellyn Publications,

Smith, Steven R. *Wylundt's Book of Incense.* York Beach, ME: Samuel Weiser, Inc. 1989.

Tyson, Donald. *Three Books of Occult Philosophy.* St. Paul: Llewelllyn publications, 1993.

Underhill, Callia. *A Witch's Book of Divination.* St. Paul: Llewelllyn publications, 1996.

Webster, Richard. *Omens, Oghams & Oracles.* St. Paul: Llewellyn Publications, 1995.

Helping Yourself With Selected Prayers. Bronx, New York: Original Publications, 1988.

Saint Joseph Edition, The New American Bible. New York: Catholic Book Publishing Co. 1987.

Holy Bible, New International Version. Grand Rapids, MI: Zondervan Bible Publishers, 1983.

SUGGESTED READING FOR FURTHER STUDY

Author's Note: The books listed below will help you conduct a deeper study of the material covered in this book.

Helping Yourself With Selected Prayers.
> Available in Spanish or English. To obtain a copy of this book write to Original Publications, Original Products Co., Dept. H. 2486-88 Webster Ave., Bronx, New York. 10458. Ph. (212) 367–9589.

Practical Candleburning Rituals and *Advanced Candle Magick* by Ray Buckland (Llewellyn Publications, 1982 and 1996).

Mountain Magick: Folk Magick & Wisdom from the Heart of Appalachia by Edain McCoy (Llewellyn Publications, 1997).

Hex Craft: Dutch Country Pow-Pow Magick by Silver Ravenwolf (Llewellyn Publications, 1995).

Folkways by Patricia Telesco (Llewellyn Publications, 1995).

The Candle Magick Workbook by Kala & Ketz Pajeon (Citadel Press, 1991).

Cunningham's Encyclopedia of Magical Herbs by Scott Cunningham (Llewellyn Publications, 1985).

Complete Book of Incense, Oils, and Brews by Scott Cunningham (Llewellyn Publications, 1989).

Buckland's Complete Gypsy Fortuneteller by Raymond Buckland (Llewellyn Publications, 1989).

The Rune Oracle Kit by Silver Ravenwolf (Llewellyn Publications, 1996).

Victorian Flower Oracle by Patricia Telesco (Llewellyn Publications, 1994).

Omens, Oghams & Oracles by Richard Webster (Llewellyn Publications, 1995).

Secrets of Gypsy Fortunetelling by Raymond Buckland (Llewellyn Publications, 1988).

Incense by Leo Vinci (publisher not available, 1980).

Wylundt's Book of Incense by Steven R. Smith (Samuel Weiser, 1996).

INDEX

LOOK FOR THE CRESCENT MOON

Llewellyn publishes hundreds of books on your favorite subjects! To get these exciting books, including the ones on the following pages, check your local bookstore or order them directly from Llewellyn.

ORDER BY PHONE
- Call toll-free within the U.S. and Canada, 1-800-THE MOON
- In Minnesota, call (612) 291-1970
- We accept VISA, MasterCard, and American Express

ORDER BY PHONE
- Send the full price of your order (MN residents add 7% sales tax) in U.S. funds, plus postage & handling to:

  Llewellyn Worldwide
  P.O. Box 64383, Dept. (K 456–1)
  St. Paul, MN 55164–0383, U.S.A.

POSTAGE & HANDLING
(For the U.S., Canada, and Mexico)
- $4.00 for orders $15.00 and under
- $5.00 for orders over $15.00
- No charge for orders over $100.00

We ship UPS in the continental United States. We ship standard mail to P.O. boxes. Orders shipped to Alaska, Hawaii, The Virgin Islands, and Puerto Rico are sent first-class mail. Orders shipped to Canada and Mexico are sent surface mail.

International orders: Airmail—add freight equal to price of each book to the total price of order, plus $5.00 for each non-book item (audio tapes, etc.). **Surface mail**—Add $1.00 per item.

Allow 4–6 weeks for delivery on all orders.
Postage and handling rates subject to change.

DISCOUNTS
We offer a 20% discount to group leaders or agents. You must order a minimum of 5 copies of the same book to get our special quantity price.

FREE CATALOG
Get a free copy of our color catalog, *New Worlds of Mind and Spirit.* Subscribe for just $10.00 in the United States and Canada ($30.00 overseas, airmail). Many bookstores carry *New Worlds*—ask for it!

Visit our web site at www.llewellyn.com for more information.

CHARMS, SPELLS AND
FORMULAS

For the Making and Use of
Gris Gris Bags, Herb Candles,
Doll Magic, Incenses,
Oils and Powders

Ray Malbrough

Hoodoo magick is a blend of European techniques and the magick
brought to the New World by slaves from Africa. Now you can learn
the methods which have been used successfully by Hoodoo practitioners for nearly 200 years.

By using the simple materials available in nature, you can bring
about the necessary changes to greatly benefit your life and that of
your friends. You are given detailed instructions for making and
using the "gris-gris" (charm) bags only casually or mysteriously mentioned by other writers. Malbrough not only shows you how to make
gris-gris bags for health, money, luck, love and protection from evil
and harm, but he also explains how these charms work. He also
takes you into the world of doll magick to gain love, success, or prosperity. Complete instructions are given for making the dolls and
setting up the ritual.

0-87542-501-1, 192 pp., 5¼ x 8, illus., softcover   **$6.95**

To order, Call 1–800–THE–MOON.

Prices subject ot change without notice.

ADVANCED CANDLE MAGICK

**More Spells and Rituals
for Every Purpose**

Ray Buckland

Seize control of your destiny with the simple but profound practice of *Advanced Candle Magick.* Ray Buckland's first book on candle magick—Practical Candleburning Rituals—explained the basic techniques of directing positive forces and "making things happen." In *Advanced Candle Magick,* you'll use advanced spells, preparatory work, visualization and astrology to improve and enhance your results. Create a framework conducive to potent spellwork through the use of planetary hours, days of the week, herb and stone correspondences, and color symbolism. Create positive changes in your relationships, finances, health and spirit when you devise your own powerful rituals based upon the sample spells presented in this book. Taking spellworking one step further, Ray Buckland gives you what you've been waiting for: *Advanced Candle Magick.*

1-56718-103-1, 5¼ x 8, 280 pp., illus., softcover $12.95